THE TAO OF MEDITATION
Way to Enlightenment

Jou, Tsung Hwa

坐
靜
開
悟
之
道

Tai Chi Foundation

Parts of Chapter §4-1 meditation on daily life are copyrighted by Shoshana Shapiro, Ph.D. and reprinted here with her permission.

First Printing in Taiwan March 1983

Third Printing in Taiwan January 1986

Fifth Printing in Taiwan December 1991

Sixth Printing June 2000

ISBN 0-8048-1465-1

Published by

Tai Chi Foundation

7199 E. Shea Blvd. Ste 109-225

Scottsdale, AZ 85254

Dedicated to:

Tai Chi Foundation

THE TAO SERIES
by Jou, Tsung Hwa

1. **The Tao of Tai Chi Chuan**

   Way to Rejuvenation

   Third revised edition

2. **The Tao of Meditation**

   Way to Enlightenment

   Shows you how to open your mind and spirit. For the frist time in English, the Way to enlightenment

3. **The Tao of I Ching**

   Way to Divination

   A new and refreshing way to understand and utilize the I Ching.

I enjoy meditating in the mountain,
time seems to roll back.
The pine tree casts a green shadow,
white clouds turn slowly.

....

In Portland,Oregon

The majestic Big Buddha （彰化大佛） meditates on the Eight Trigrams Hill （八卦山） in Changhua, a county in central Taiwan. Like the Statue of Liberty, a staircase inside this huge statue allows visitors to climb to his head and look through the Buddha's eyes-- seeing a great distance. Thousands of pilgrims come to offer incense to Buddha and visit the temple located next to the statue.

Kuan Yin（觀音）, the Goddess of Mercy, uses her great powers to show love and charity to all the needy people in the world. Many families have Kuan Yin's picture in their homes, and pray daily to her by chanting her name. Kuan Yin's "Boat of Mercy" will take all those who live a life of charity into the bliss of paradise.

Buddha with Five Kids（五子佛）is located next to Kuan Yin's statue on a small hill in Chang San Park in Keelung,（基隆）the north port city of Taiwan. His smiling face looking out on the beautiful harbor reminds visitors to not take life too seriously, transferring his joy to them. To understand how huge this statue is, consider that the five kids are larger than a normal adult!

CONTENTS

CONTENTS

INTRODUCTION

Nature, or what the Chinese call the Tao, has been both kind and fair to all of us. We have received not only the gift of life but when we look closely, we find that each of us has received a unique collection of talents and strengths to use in making the most of our lives.

What have we, in this modern age, sought to achieve with our natural gifts? Perhaps we seek money to live comfortably or advancement and authority or high achievements of various sorts. Perhaps we simply seek that modest, but noble, purpose: "to be a good person."

Yet how often do we feel that we are cheating ourselves and somehow missing the point of all we strive for and suffer to achieve? We have read of the billionaire who sacrificed his entire life to become rich and now walks from room to room in his huge mansion shutting off lights to save a few pennies. He can not even relax and enjoy his great riches. Are we, even with our much smaller fortunes, just like this billionaire? Perhaps we have attained our material goals. Yet, we often find ourselves tired, frustrated, and neglectful of important matters in our personal life. We lose track of our personal dreams, until, like the poet Wordsworth, we cry out:

> The world is too much with us; late and soon,
> Getting and spending, we lay waste our powers;

Little we see in Nature that is ours;
We have given our hearts away, a sordid boon!

How can we discover those gifts which nature bestows on each one of us? An aptitude test, employment test, I.Q. test, or even psychological testing cannot reveal these special gifts to us. At best, those types of tests only estimate our ability to conform to society's standards of behavior and intelligence. These standards come from outside ourselves.

We must look within ourselves, not once, but again, and again, and again, to discover those things about ourselves that are most important to us. At first, even a small amount of progress will require much time, especially if we have neglected the practice of "looking within" in the past. The greater the confusion and disorganization we have stored inside ourselves through aimless, undirected living, the more work there will be to clear it away. However, it is not a task to ignore, no matter how insurmountable it may seem. For looking within ourselves is the most important thing we can do to learn how to live well. As we do this, we begin to use meditation for its highest purpose: to do something genuinely good for ourselves and for other people.

The Chinese term for meditation is Ching Tso (靜坐), which translated means "sitting still with a peaceful mind." Meditation is the training of the inner senses of the body and mind. It is as rigorous as the training undertaken by an athlete or an artist.

I began meditating in the form of Tai Chi Chuan, which is meditation in motion as well as a martial art and a healing art. Two years after I began the practice of Tai Chi, I added Ching Tso, which has proved to be an invaluable aid in studying and extending the mastery of Tai Chi Chuan.

My own experience in seeking literature on the art of meditation made me aware that very little information is available, either here or in China. The ancient Chinese works are written in a language that is now as archaic to the speaker of modern Chinese as Chaucerian English is to the speaker of modern American English. The information is made even more obscure by the frequent use of metaphors to communicate experiences that are difficult to put into words. As a result, even a person whose native language is Chinese cannot understand the information with special training. For English-speaking people, it is nearly impossible to find a book that clearly describes these traditional methods.

Yet, these traditional works are not just writings on ancient history to be studied by Chinese scholars. They are living documents which can help us in our personal development in modern times. These traditional works were developed and refined over countless generations by people who were as puzzled and concerned as we are about the nature of life and how to best live our lives.

For example, Ching Tso (meditation) is not a religion, yet it can help all people of all religions. By helping us to think clearly and concentrate fully, Ching Tso enables us to commune totally with our God, without distracting or artificial thoughts. These ancient writings tell us that if we indulge in evil deeds or gain profit for ourselves at the expense of others, we cannot find favor with our God. The true purpose of meditation is to develop ourselves and our relationship to all of life. I have kept in mind this concern for life while writing this book.

Although science has made many advances in our modern age, to use scientific knowledge to understand meditation is, as the Chinese proverb says, "To scratch itching foot with the boot on." We can imagine that all our human knowledge is a building with many windows. Each window gives a different and valuable view of life. Science is a window. Philosophy is a window. Religion, Psychology, Physiology, and all other fields of study are windows. As long as we continue looking out of these windows, we will never get outside. We will never have the chance to look at this building in which we live. No matter how much knowledge we gain, we are still "looking through windows."

Our perception of time is limited. The past only exists for us because we all share a biological organism that perceives and retains impression of three-dimensional events. Our present, although an abstract continuous process, does not really exist for us because it immediately becomes the past as soon as we perceive it. The future exists only in our imaginations. We do not know what will happen in the future.

The highest and most advanced goal of meditation is to gain enlightenment. We want to go beyond the limitations of our knowledge and our three-dimensional view of the world. Our goal is to perceive fully the fourth dimension and understand our relationship to it.

It is my hope that this book will fulfill the need for a practical work on the philosophical background and the practice of meditation. It is a guide for anyone who wants to enter the realm of personal development and enlightenment that is possible through meditation.

Meditation has a paradoxical quality. If we succeed in reaching a particular kind of inner experience, then we shall understand it. But, if we have not yet reached that level, then no amount of explanation and description will ever make us understand it. Thus, the exercises in this book do not include any explanation beyond that which is necessary for us to practice them correctly. These exercises have been passed on to us by people much like ourselves as a means to develop inner awareness.

Simply reading these exercises will tell us nothing. But practicing them will enable each of us to become our own "sage" and to develop a path of communion with the Tao that each of us is offered by life.

In the ancient Chinese writing, Tao Te Ching by Lao Tzu, we can read words that are still true today. A person who talks all the time knows nothing. The person who truly knows things, talks very little. Perhaps I am talking too much about meditation, and in that sense I really do not know much about meditation myself.

There are a number of people who have been helpful in the writing of this book. Without their advice, assistance, and encouragement, writing this book would have been much more difficult.

I would especially like to thank the following: James Birney, Jay Dunbar, Hess, Paul Albe, Zollo, Louis Kovi, Linda Lustig, Bruce Ballai, Victor Franco. And, I extend a very special gratitude to Mindy Sheps for her work with me during a period of about three months! Also I appreciate the drawings by my student Wang Chien-Chang (王建章) who has expended much time and talent.

Jou, Tsung Hwa.
March, 3rd. 1983.

第　一　章

陰陽與太極

Yin-Yang
and
Tai-Chi

🮑 1-1 Yin-Yang and Tai-Chi

The ancient Chinese philosophers used the concept known as Yin and Yang to describe all the properties of the universe, which in turn explain the nature of creation and existence. The realization of a way, or natural order of universal peace and harmony, was likewise made clear through the study of Yin and Yang.

We might ask how two words, Yin and Yang, can possibly represent the properties or complexities of the universe. To understand the answer to this question, let us look at a simple mathematics operation. Everyone knows that one apple plus two apples equals three apples. The procedure can be done with any objects, whether they are pencils, books, persons, or whatever. In repeating this process with diverse sets of like objects, it soon becomes apparent that there is a common process. This process may be identified and described quite independently of the types of objects used. This idea of abstracting the relation of quantity involved in every case is illustrated below:

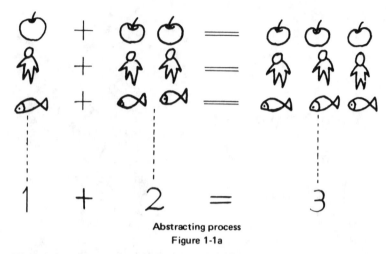

Abstracting process
Figure 1-1a

This is an example of generalizing from the particular. This idea which has proved so useful in organizing scientific knowledge, is readily applied to the principle of duality. Duality deals with the intimate relationship that binds opposites together. It is pervasive in nature, as with night and day, down and up, cold and hot, soft and hard, west and east, and so on. In Chinese philosophy this universally applicable principle of duality is called Yin and Yang. A simple way of using it is illustrated below by a set of paired opposites, and their separation as shown in figure 1-1b.

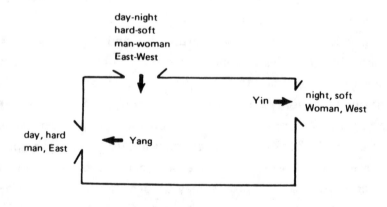

Abstracting Machine
Figure 1-1b

In other contexts, pairings of Yin and Yang include such concepts as start-finish, negative-positive, extrovert-introvert, and material-spiritual. The pairings of Yin and Yang remind us of two distinct aspects in understanding any duality: (1) distinguishing the opposites, and (2) recognizing the nature of the dynamics that relate one with the other. The dynamics relating Yin and Yang may be characterized as an all-pervasive, alternating, complementary and temporal relationship between them. Each pole or member implies the other and their energies move in a continuous, cyclic ebb and flow relationship.

In the Hebrew Kabala mysticism, the numbers from one through ten and the twenty-two Hebrew alphabetic characters are used to symbolize the Divine, or the whole of the spiritual world. The ten numbers in this system symbolize the following five dualities:

1:	The start of the infinite	2:	Its end
3:	Good	4:	Evil
5:	Height	6:	Depth
7:	East	8:	West
9:	South	10:	North

This list is readily seen to be selective and not all-inclusive. According to Yin-Yang philosophy, we can see that the Yin and Yang duality is at once more compact and all-encompassing; in fact, it is limitless.

In dealing with the concept of numbers and their relationships, it is instructive to distinguish natural numbers from man-made ones. In this context, natural numbers are taken to be the minimum set needed, from which we may construct all the rest. The mathematician Leopold Kronecker (1823-1891) declared, "God made the integers, all else is the work of man." However, even the set of integers includes more elements than necessary to form the desired basics. In particular, all negative integers are derived from their positive counterparts by the use of a man-made principle. The property of additive inverses, which holds that the sum of any number and its opposite is zero, codifies that relationship. A further refinement was made in 1899 by the Italian

mathematician Guiseppi Peano. He introduced three undefined terms;
the unit, the number, and the successor, to create an axiomatic system
consisting of five postulates as a sound basis for the development of
number theory.   Peano postulated that the number one is the unit
which is the least element, that every element has a successor (one has
as a successor two, two has three, etc.) and defined the rules for
addition and multiplication. The number one is thus recognized to be
basic, and so qualifies as natural. In mathematical systems, postulates
and axioms are assumptions that serve as a basis for developing a
mathematical structure. Being assumptions, they are amenable neither
to proof nor to the search for a more basic origin. When philosophizing
about the reality of daily life, we may inquire into the origin of the
number one.   Where does it fit in relation to the other numbers?   If
one were to locate it on the number line, it would seem to be "lost" by
itself as shown in figure 1-1c. Without a point of reference, its position
on the number line would be meaningless. The number zero provides
such a reference, and its relationship to one defines both the positive
direction and the unit distance.

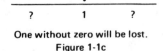

One without zero will be lost.
Figure 1-1c

Peano's axioms apply to the so-called natural, or counting
numbers, which do not include a zero. In this system, zero is the
additive identity element, and one is the multiplicative identity; that is,
for any number a,

$$a + 0 = a \qquad \text{and} \qquad a \cdot 1 = a.$$

It appears then that both zero and one, and no other numbers,
are required to form a basis for creating all other numbers. They are
natural in the desired sense. In relating this dichotomy to the idea of
Yin and Yang, zero is the beginning and end of existence, which is Yin,
and the number one represents unity, or Yang. The numbers zero and
one thus are abstracted to Yin and Yang. This is reflected in the fact
that computers use only zero and one. Computers use an abstraction

process to represent all the concepts in reality, that is similar to the Chinese philosophers use of Yin and Yang. On this basis, computers can solve all quantitative problems, thus allowing for the possibility of solving any problems.

In the example of the computer, it is easy to see that while the computer is man-made or artificial, it still corresponds to that which is not man-made, but which has objectively real existence. This correspondence can help us understand many things, and especially can aid us in comprehending what may be the source of all creative occurrences in the cosmos. From studying and thinking about the creative process as it is actualized by man, we can next begin to study and think about the creative process as it occurs naturally in the cosmos.

What is most important about these two areas of study is that we begin to learn to distinguish between what is man-made and what is natural in ourselves. This is the direct road to enlightenment in meditation. We must distinguish between the artificial clutter and the natural contents of our minds so that we may successfully remove the clutter and rediscover our basic nature. A central tenet of Eastern philosophy is that the natural state of man is enlightenment. Only that which we have unnecessarily created stands between ourselves and enlightenment.

We are all very familiar with this confusion of the subjective and the objective because it is seen in our daily lives as the unfortunate situation that our various religions find themselves in. Many people ask, "Why are more and more churches and temples losing their congregations?" or "Why don't the young people want to attend services?" We can now see that these problems are a result of the great difficulty in distinguishing the man-made or artificial from the objectively real in religion.

All the great religions have certain things in common such as the concept of a creator, the need to love all people and treat them as brothers and sisters, and the desirability of peace. These can be seen as the natural or objective aspects of the religions. They are the things which everyone needs and which can really help mankind. The differences between these religions is in the man-made or artificial things such as the structure of the temple, or the ceremonial clothes, or the ceremony itself. The fact that not as many people are enthusiastic about religions as were in the past is obvious, so people try to change the religions for the better. But because great care is not taken to distinguish between the natural and the man-made, often times the changes made are such that the useful objective aspects are lost, and only the artificial clutter remains. This of course makes us even more unhappy so it must be changed again and again. Since there is no discrimination between what is artificial and what is natural in religions, no real solution comes. Perhaps if the great leaders of the world's great religions could sit and meditate together upon what is artificial and what is natural in each of their religions, they could then make the necessary changes so that the great religions would come into correspondence with objective reality. Such a situation could start with a simple task. Each religion has a different name for the Creator. What does this mean and what can we learn from this? The Creator is part of the objective, but the different names are subjective, or man-made. We should not argue about what name to call the Creator, or who has the "right" name, or insult another religion's name. What we should do is realize that we all believe in a Creator, and then, with open minds, learn from one another all points of view about the Creator instead of calling each other "pagans" or "unbelievers."

We do not argue about the words we use to count with in different languages, but instead learn, if necessary, the different names. Numbers are the same whether you call them one, two, three, or uno, dos, tres or Ee, Er, San. The binary counting system is still the binary counting system whether we build a computer in America or a computer in China. They are both built upon the binary counting system and are both in correspondence with the natural, objective reality of the binary system.

That everyone wants computers is self-evident. They work according to a natural principle even though they are man-made. If the great religions of the world could be brought into correspondence with their natural principles, then everyone would want them. Everyone wants a computer since it makes our work easier. Everyone would want a religion if it would make our lives fuller.

Almost three thousand years ago, Lao-Tzu (primary exponent of the Chinese philosophy of Taoism) revealed this truth:

> The way, or Tao, begot one,
> And the one, two,
> Then the two begot three,
> And the three, all else.

Thus, the Tao can be considered the way of nature. Religious men have called the source of creation God, and science endeavors to discover the laws governing relationships occurring in nature. However, neither religion nor science can encompass, define, or fully describe the sources, the Tao itself. Thus, the Tao can neither be put into words nor proven. Among primitive peoples in any era, the phenomenon of thunder and lightening was seen to be a part of the Tao because there was no satisfactory explanation for its occurrence. Religious leaders readily interpreted thunder and lightening in terms of God's punishment for his wayward people. Eventually science progressed to the point where these phenomena could be explained as electrostatic reactions that, given particular weather conditions, would occur naturally in the atmosphere. However, once a rationale for any event was generally accepted, on whatever grounds, scientific, religious, or other, these events were no longer a part of the Tao. Whenever something is understood, explained, or can be rationalized by the mind, the idea of the Tao is no longer applicable, because the Tao represents that which is completely beyond comprehension. More importantly, so much more always remains to be explained, and each new discovery raises more questions than it answers, so that the Tao can be said to exist everywhere. In this sense, the Tao includes everything.

It is intriguing to speculate upon the question of how, as in Lao-Tzu's verse, the Tao begot one. How did we get from a state of non-existence to that of existence, from zero to one? Consider what happens to the mind at rest in a zero state without any thought. A thought suddenly appears spontaneously. Just how this happens is obscure, but we note that the mind is no longer at rest. This critical transitional moment, prior to which the mind was in a state of nothingness, or Wu-Chi, is said to be the moment that the state of Tai-Chi or the grand terminus starts. Tai-Chi is the state of fullness or activity which includes all the events that go into the dynamic interplay of the Tao. For this event, from no thought to thought, the Chinese have the expression "from Wu-Chi to Tai-Chi" The state of Tai-Chi starts at the point of transition and may be represented by a step function on the time axis as shown in figure 1-1d:

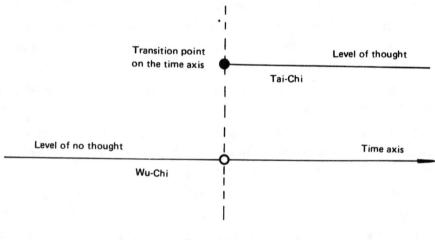

Figure 1-1d

In the energy flow of life, Wu-Chi can be said to represent the past, Tai-Chi the future, and the moment of transition the timeless present. By transferring this idea to the spatial framework of the universe, we can think of the universal void prior to its creation as being in the state of Wu-Chi. The void was followed by a manifestly substantive universe, one in the state of Tai-Chi. The question arises, how does a universe transform from the void to a created universe?

This is the same question as that related to the spontaneous appearance of a thought. In the present state of knowledge, we can only say that there must be an instant in which the transition from nothing to something occurs. The something may be characterized as a geometric point. There is no way to describe or locate the point, as it occupies an infinitesimally small space, yet all space is comprised entirely of such points.

Chinese philosophy depicts the Tao in terms of the Tai-Chi diagram as shown in the figure 1-1e:

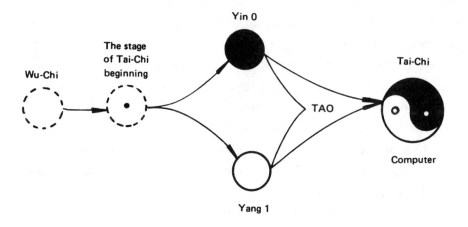

Figure 1-1e

The figure represents the dynamic relationship as an alternating circular movement. Picture a rotating vector hinged at the center, sweeping out changing complementary areas of Yin and Yang. This applies to all opposites that occur in nature and in human experience. For example, the Yang represents day and Yin night. Their duality as opposites is clear enough. If the alternating between opposites is upset and balance is lost, the result is the type of conditions we find in life today. Many people understand now that certain man-made things are not positive, or that the results of man-made things are not good for them. For instance, we have developed technology and industry for the sake of making a more comfortable, fuller life. Yet the results have not been quite as we predicted. People are much more comfortable. No one will deny the comfort and attractiveness of air conditioning, or central heat. But the cost of this comfort has now after a hundred years become perhaps too much for us to pay. Air pollution, water pollution, food pollution, radiation, animals poisoned and faced with extinction, food shortages, and many other uncomfortable situations are turning up as "bills past due." Why is this? This is simply the result of any man-made, or subjective activity, as opposed to the natural, or objective occurrence. The natural always occurs as part of a dynamic balance which swings back and forth but maintains an equilibrium. How could the men of technology foresee the air pollution the factories would make? They could not see the air pollution then since there were very few factories at first, and why would they think any farther ahead than today's profits? After all they were only men dealing in their newly created "man-made world." They did not learn from nature and try to apply natural principles to their factories. If they had done this they would have watched and seen how when there are too many rabbits in an area, more fox and bobcat appear to feed on and reduce this excessive population. When too many deer are feeding in a forest either more wolves come in or the food runs out and the deer starve to death, and balance is restored. So, if we would find principles that may be applied to ourselves to give positive, long-lasting results, we must look to the natural way and either bring the man-made into correspondence with it or cast it out.

Perhaps this "artificial man-made" technology is really the result of a natural law, and is just a method of restoring balance in nature by causing a self-destroying tendency to appear in man, since he does not seem to want to bring himself into harmony with the rest of nature. In an objectively natural life no one side would be acceptable, but all points of view would be balanced, making everything natural in combination. A balanced state of opposites would not let atomic energy be developed as a method of war and destruction, but it would not refuse to use atomic energy. It would use atomic energy only in a safe, productive, and positive way, balancing all advantages and disadvantages so as to create a harmonious action. There is no lasting extreme Yin or Yang in a natural state since such a situation eventually destroys itself and balance is then restored.

More subtle, but equally important, is the way in which the cyclic alternating flow from one state to the other reveals their mutually dependent relationship as an essential characteristic that insures harmony and stability for this, or any other dualistic system. Each implies the other, just as in the diagram there is a little Yin in the Yang, and vice versa. The sun at its zenith signals the beginning of sunset, and the coldest day in winter is also the first in a return to warmer days. Yin flows into Yang and back again, forever. Man must learn that he cannot survive without accepting change and adapting to it, along the natural path.

1-2 The Riddle of Creation

Since time immemorial, mankind has been concerned with the fundamental questions of life. The first of these, "Where do we come from?" goes back not only to the creation of mankind, but more generally to the creation of the universe itself.

Various cultures and religions have evolved distinct ideas about creation, which is an instance of the Tao. In recent times, philosophers, scientists, and particularly astronomers have developed various theories to explain the origin of the universe. Although current theories seem very sophisticated, at least in comparison to the primitive idea that the earth was obviously a flat surface and the sky above in the shape of a hemisphere, a question arises. How far have we come, and how much further can we go, toward filling out a completely satisfying picture? Metaphorically speaking, what is taught about astronomy in graduate school today is far beyond the simple concepts that the mind of a child in elementary school can grasp. Likewise, what will be known in, say, one, two, or ten generations hence will be far beyond today's concepts, which will belong to the elementary curriculum in the schools of the

future.   By providing an elementary school type example, we can
perhaps begin to appreciate the nature and scope of the problems
related to solving the riddle of creation.

On April 1, 1978, I attended a Tai-Chi workshop in Florida. It
was a beautiful Saturday morning. Sitting on the patio, I began to
reflect on the attractive courtyard and surrounding structure. How did
it come into being?   How was it created from nothing into this
beauti'ul structure? First, the idea had to be born in the mind of the
creato r, whoever he or she might have been. This process represents the
transition from Wu-Chi to Tai-Chi, as shown in figure 1-2a:

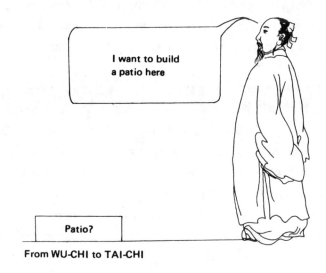

From WU-CHI to TAI-CHI

Figure 1-2a

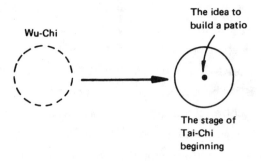

Based on his or her life experience and prodded by ambition and imagination, the creator of this idea conceptualized the overall design as appropriate to its locale; that is, he began to see the completed structure in his mind's eye. First, he envisioned its general appearance, size, and construction materials. As the idea became more attractive, he thought more and more about the many details involved, such as the arrangement of rooms, size, shape, location of windows, wiring, plumbing, flooring, furnishings, and so forth. After completing all these details, the creator had developed the real structure in his mind. This completed mental creation defines the Yin aspect, or the soul, of the real patio. This is shown in figure 1-2b:

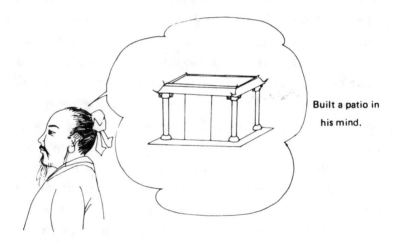

Built a patio in
his mind.

The Yin aspect of a patio.

Figure 1-2b

Since no one can see it, it is called the Yin aspect of the patio. Only the creator knows of it.

The Yin aspect may be combined with other Yin aspects just as a child's blocks might be assembled. This might occur, for instance, when a house is built by one person, and a patio added on by another. In this case, the Yin aspect of the home and the Yin aspect of the patio

were created by different people at different times, but now these two
Yin aspects are connected and form the Yin aspect of the home and
patio as a whole unit.

The Yin aspect can also transfer its operation from one agent to
another. For example, someone can transfer his or her idea of a patio,
or Yin aspect, to a specialist in patios who will then develop the Yin
aspect further before the patio is built. This kind of process could,
in fact, become a progression from the creator to architect to builder
to subcontractor to painter and so forth.

The manifestation of a Yin aspect may be multiple, which means
the same Yin aspect may appear in separate places in different ways.
For example, the Yin aspect of a canal might be manifested at one time
and place through certain people as the Suez Canal, and also appear at
another time and place and built by other people as the Panama Canal.

It is important to understand that the Yin aspect is not static. It is
dynamic. It is, in motion at some time. For instance, when Watt
observed a tea kettle always with steam escaping he wondered how this energy
could be harnessed and used. This was the Yin aspect of what was later
to become a steam engine. At first, however, it was only a simple desire
to utilize the energy. It moved and changed over time to become the
Yin aspect of Watt's engine. In fact, this movement of the Yin aspect is
as dynamic as growth, and we can say that the Yin aspect is born,
grows, and dies. When the Yin aspect does not manifest itself in our
world, it is like the bamboo shoot that dies while still under the ground.
It never breaks through to appear above ground as a full grown
bamboo. This can be experienced when we have an idea in mind but
cannot carry it out. A person might make the decision to be a
musician, but if he or she cannot practice and study music every day,
the idea remains as only a Yin aspect and is never carried out, just as
the bamboo shoot dies before it breaks through the ground. There is
also the case of the Yin aspect that grows and changes as a dynamic
entity. For example, a great inventor, while mapping the plan of an
idea, sees another application of the same idea and draws another plan,

and while drawing that one, sees another application, and so on. This is a Yin aspect that is in dynamic growth such as the Yin aspect of the hundreds of inventions of Thomas Edison.

The next step in building the patio is to set the idea down on paper in blueprint form. The initial idea of doing that represents another transition from Wu-Chi to Tai-Chi. The creator can either do this by himself or have a draftsman do it for him. Once the drawings are completed, other people can, for the first time, see what was originally in the mind of the creator. The completed drawings represent the Yang aspect on the paper in the two-dimensional world of length and width as shown in the figure 1-2c.

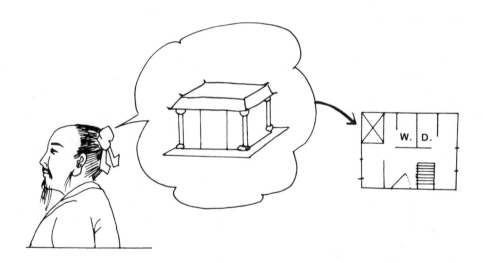

The transition of Yin aspect into Yang aspect in a two-dimensional world.
Figure 1-2c

This change from concept or mental world to the plane drawings indicates the first transition from the Yin aspect of the patio projected to the Yang aspect in the two-dimensional world. Another example would be a child drawing on the wall with a crayon, the hand loosely guided by the Yin aspect in his mind, where the shapes he has seen are translated into simple circles and lines. Painters, artists, and novelists work regularly to project their Yin aspect into a two-dimensional world.

Once the plans are completed, the work of bringing the structure, or the Yang aspect, into the three-dimensional world of length, width, and height begins. The ground-breaking, which may be done with or without a commemorating ceremony, represents another change from Wu-Chi to Tai-Chi. The subsequent creation of the structure, the outfitting, furnishing, landscaping, and so forth, that are needed to make the original idea into a reality represent the second transition from the Yin to the Yang aspect of the real patio in three dimensions as shown in figure 1-2d.

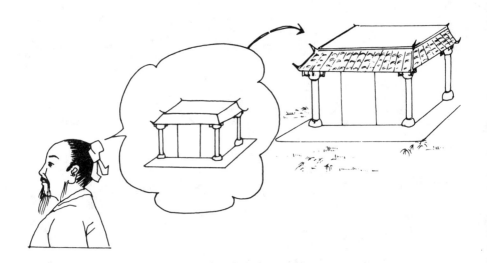

I built the patio!

The Yin aspect is projected into the Yang aspect of the real patio.
Figure 1-2d

The idea of relating the Yin aspect and the Yang aspect of a patio can be extended to other man-made objects. For example, consider any table. First, the idea of the table occurs in the mind of its creator. This represents the Yin aspect, or soul of the table. No one else can know what it is at this stage. Then the creator projects his vision, or Yin aspect, of the table onto a set of drawings, if needed. The existence of such plans represents the Yang aspect in the two-dimensional world. When the table is eventually built and thus manifested in the universe in its final form, it represents the Yin aspect projected into its full three-dimensional Yang aspect of the table as shown in the figure 1-2e.

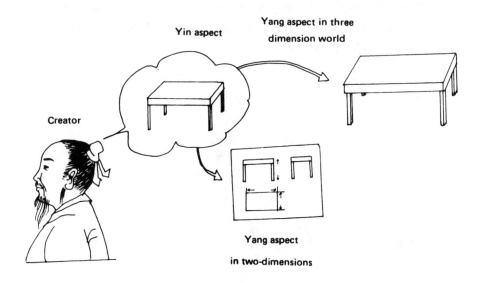

Figure 1-2e

From the examples of man-made objects, such as the patio and table, illustrating their Yin and Yang aspects, we can see that all objects of creation have a Yin aspect and a Yang aspect. We can also consider this relationship as observed in nature. Consider, for example, the rose in its origin, development, and culmination. The plant develops from the seed. As the rosebush grows and flourishes, buds appear which blossom into the full flower in all its visual beauty and olfactory excellence. All we can see is the Yang aspect of the rose. Does someone design a rose as one does a patio or table, starting with its original conception in the mind? With its life cycle and sensual aspects, particularly its physical beauty and its exquisite and delicate scent, the rose is but one form of the variety of flowers that exist. Flowers come in many sizes, ranging from very tiny to quite large. The variety of floral forms found in nature staggers the imagination. In contemplating this variety, can we believe that these myriad manifestations of nature could come about automatically? Do they just appear without rhyme or reason? Where did they come from? Who designed such exquisite flowers? See figure 1-2f.

Who designed the Yin aspect of the rose?
Figure 1-2f

Religions assert that such creation is the handiwork of God. Science has attempted to explore the truth. Therefore, it is reasonable to say that it is a part of the Tao.

Going beyond physical objects, the Yin aspect and Yang aspect can be extended to movements or processes, such as Tai-Chi Chuan or basketball games that people play every day. For example, the idea, or Yin aspect comes first. It is created by someone. Rules are developed and are used to direct the corresponding human action. The actual exercise or game that people can see or experience represents the Yang aspect of that exercise.

With respect to the process of planetary motion in the solar system, the Yang aspect, as observable through the telescope, refers to the actual motion of these bodies. The Yin aspect of planetary motion has been codified in Kepler's law of planetary motion as follows:

1. The planet's orbits are ellipses with the sun at one focus.

2. The planets in their motion around the sun sweep out equal areas in equal times as shown in the figure 1-2g.

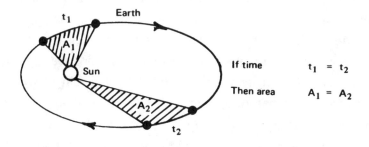

Figure 1-2g

3. The centripetal force of gravitational attraction between sun and planet varies inversely as the square of the distance and this is true for any one or for all planets.

We cannot say with finality that this knowledge comprises the totality of the Yin aspect of planetary motion. The fact that these laws are obeyed is verified by observation over extended time periods and, therefore, extrapolated with accuracy into the future. It is a very important point which means that *we can, to some extent, communicate with our Creator.* Any theory, principle, or law relating to particular physical or mental processes represent the Yin aspect, and the discovery or invention of such laws and processes is in fact merely the ability to "read" the message which is present in all things. What else can this be called but communication between mankind and creator? If I write a letter to you in Chinese, you will not be able to accept my communication until you can read Chinese. The process will take even longer if you are illiterate, and must first develop literacy. So it is in terms of relating to the Yin aspect of things. Once the Yin aspect can be recognized, it is then necessary to learn how to "read" it.

To recognize the Yin aspect of things we must first determine what sort of correspondence the Yin aspect has to the Yang aspect. In man-made things, especially mass produced items, the Yin aspect is to the Yang aspect as a one to many correspondence, since the same Yin aspect is duplicated in each item. This is in fact the goal of most man-made processes, to produce a large quantity of identical Yang aspects from one Yin aspect. In natural processes, however, there is a one to one correspondence, since the Yin aspect of each river is unique, just as each river is unique; and no two mountains are the same, etc. Man now creates in mass as an imitation of living beings, which are the only things which nature apparently "mass produces." However, we learn just how false this apparent similarity is, when we try to have a discussion with someone we thought was just like us, only to find out that there is no similarity at all!

Man does create in a natural way, however, whenever an individual creates one complete individual object. When a craftsman of two hundred years ago made beds, each bed was different, since he started from nothing and did not stop until the individual bed was completed. So it also must be with the actualization of the Yin aspect of natural things.

Despite this analogy, it may still seem difficult to see and comprehend the process of Yin aspect growing into Yang aspect, or the correspondence of the two aspects, or even the existence of the Yin aspect. Therefore consider as another example what happens when we hear a piece of music. The music exists only in the perception of our hearing and the time of our memory. It is a man-made creation which is not three-dimensional or even two-dimensional, but is actually dimensionless. Yet the music does exist and we can be sure it has a Yin aspect, since some person had to think of this melody first. How then can we discount the existence of the Yin aspect of all natural creation?

So, with respect to the general problem of the riddle of creation, we can reasonably assume that for the objects, processes, and events explained above — the patio, the table, the rose, the Tai-Chi Chuan, the basketball game, the planetary motion, the bed, and the music, there is both a Yin aspect and Yang aspect with the Yin aspect the necessary precursor to the projected corresponding Yang aspect.

② 1-3 Who am I?

Now let us consider the actual creation of humankind. The Yang aspect of human creation includes the uniting of sperm and egg, the prenatal development of the fetus, the actual birth, and the infant. The Yang aspect of the creation is just like the Yang aspect of the patio in that the actual building of the patio, from the architect to the painter, includes only those processes which are physical.

The metaphysical question of importance here is by whom or how was the Yin aspect of human creation developed? There are those individuals who might say that creation, birth, and so on, just "happen," with no order or plan. However, this is a casual and naive view of creation.

Consider the intricate planning and designing required to extinguish the fire of a burning house. First, the hydrant was planned and placed in a convenient location fifty or a hundred years ago, before the fire ever started. The fire engines were equipped with ladders, axes, etc. Hoses were designed to fit perfectly with the water sources, and so on. All of this preparation and master planning for fighting a fire are necessarily complex. There can be no function neglected. Even one screw threaded improperly could result in a leak which would make the entire system ineffective. Considering this simple example of fire fighting, is it logical to suggest that there was no plan, no order, for the tremendously more complex process of human creation? The Yang aspect of creation — human union, conception, and birth — is perfect in every way. Men and women are constructed to unite and complement each other's design totally. Consider just the necessary physiological changes which occur in the body of the pregnant women. Her pelvis shifts, her womb enlarges, and her breasts fill with milk. This all takes place at a given time and in perfect sequence. The process, although incredibly complex, is totally natural.

So it follows that someone or some force had a sort of master plan which arranged the phenomenal miracle of creation. Although Charles Darwin contributed the important theory of evolution, scientists are still searching for the solution to the creation question. The Taoists suggest that the creation mystery is a part of the Tao and further explanations cannot be afforded now. The reason is the same as a thousand years ago, when humans felt as they did about the lightning and thunder. Only religions have concluded in concrete terms that God was the great architect, the creator. Of course there are those who argue against this conclusion and ask, "If God created the universe, where is God? If I do not know God, I cannot believe He created the universe." This is a meager argument, however, because we could counter that question with another question: "Do you know the creator of the fire hydrant? If not, can you believe that it was in fact designed by someone?"

This "I must see it to believe it" attitude is a very ineffective measure for truth. Our eyes can only function in a very limited capacity. We cannot see far into the distance like an eagle, or find our way through the darkness like a cat. The spectrum of visibility for the human eye is limited to just a certain length and intensity of light waves. We confine our experience of the universe within tight bounds by relying on our own eyes and sensations to translate everything. Truth, then, would become an arbitrary reflection of a limited visual perception. Certainly, our perception and experience of the universe would be drastically different if, for example, we saw by way of the X-ray rather than by visible light. We would see no muscular structure and so we would accept the skeletal structure as the truth of human anatomy.

Not only is our perception of the universe limited by our vision, it is also limited by our other senses. Our idea of the world is determined by our senses and is therefore subjective. The idea of the world is different for different beings, if their senses are different. A bat perceives the world primarily through its ears. Its ears are like our eyes, and its eyes are like our ears (in a secondary position). Obviously a bat's idea of the world is totally different from ours. Who can say which one is true? The point is that any perception of the world is subjective. It is only a very small part of the whole. Although it seems clear that our senses are underdeveloped and that we are severely limited by a meager five senses, we tend to forget our limitations. In general, as human beings we have an egotistical attitude about the universe and deceive ourselves into believing that what we see, hear, feel, taste, and smell is much more than the very little we actually experience.

We have become very pompous about our technology and take great pride in our advances. Our technology, however, is only an extension of our experience of the universe and therefore still very limited. For example, consider the problem of emptying a room. In the past, we could remove the furniture and other objects from the room and call it empty. Then we learned that the room was not empty because "air" filled the room. Later we could empty the room of air by creating a vacuum but then we learned that there were still light waves and radio waves to contend with. Perhaps we could remove these elements from the room. Can we say with one hundred percent certainty that the room is now empty? It seems very possible that something could still exist in the room of which even advanced scientists are unaware.

Consider the confusion and questioning now going through our minds as a result of this simple question of how to empty a room. Now, we ask a more complex question: "Who am I?" The answer seems very obvious at first, but as we consider it more and more, it is seen to be so confusing an idea that the first question, "How can we empty a room?" becomes simple in comparison.

Your senses are part of your physical body, and yet your consciousness, or ego, a most important part of the real essential you, is dependent upon this physical body and its senses. You equate this consciousness and the resulting ego with yourself. But how can you know yourself with something as subjective and partial as your physical body and its senses? For example, when you become ill, you must go to a doctor and ask him "What is wrong with me?" It is your own body, yet you must ask someone else about it, someone who doesn't even live in it. Can you then say with a feeling of conviction that you know yourself? When a baby becomes sick, doesn't the mother, who knows more about her child than anyone else, also have to ask the doctor, "What is wrong with my child?" How can the mother then say that she knows who her child is?

Let us take another example, something we do every day. Everyday we go to sleep and we wake up. Can we understand the process of going to sleep and the process of waking up? Can we watch ourselves go to sleep and so learn the process of going to sleep? Can we observe ourselves waking up and so understand how it is that we can wake up? Should we not at least have the ability to come to some small understanding of something that we do day in and day out?

What is most amazing about our lack of self-knowledge is that in our ignorance we torture ourselves. We imprison ourselves inside a complex set of restrictions and requirements most of which are, if not merely unnecessary and artificial, often hazardous and injurious to ourselves. Would you tie a man's necktie on a bird's neck? Of course you wouldn't, unless it was your intention to injure the bird. Yet men tie an uncomfortable tie around their neck every day. Would you put high heeled shoes on a dog? Of course not, since it would deform the dog's legs. Yet every day millions of women walk around on high heeled shoes. How could you expect an animal to live a proper free life if you put it in a cage? Yet you put a cage around yourself everyday for the sake of something as artificial as money.

Not only do we not know ourselves, not only do we torture and imprison ourselves, but we even destroy ourselves! Who would not agree that worry and depression are bad for us? Yet who is there today who does not worry to the point of depression? We all know that when we are tired, we must rest if we are to help our health. But what do we do on Friday nights, after working all week at an exhausting job? We go out and party all night. If we are overweight we eat too much. We pay money which we worried ourselves half to death about for a pack of cigarettes with a health hazard warning printed on it. We drink alcoholic beverages and drive while listening to the radio news report about how many people were killed because of drunk driving.

On one hand, we do not know about ourselves; we torture and imprison ourselves; we destroy and kill ourselves. On the other hand, we are very much attracted to the body and ego. We experience pain and pleasure directly from them. This puts us in a very difficult position. It is as if we are in a trap set by the body and ego. Whatever the body and ego direct, we feel. This leaves no room, air, or space for other more fruitful possiblities. For example, if someone compliments you by saying that you are great, you automatically feel pleasure from this. But if someone criticizes you by saying that you are awful, you immediately experience pain and anger. This example is quite common and shows the human attachment to the body.

Consider another example. Three people are to share six hundred dollars. Since each person's share is two hundred, there is no problem, and no one will worry about it. But if the three people must divide seven hundred dollars among them, one person can get three hundred. In this case, someone will gain and the others will lose. This will provoke dissension between them and each person will be thinking about himself and how he can get the extra hundred dollars.

Spectator sports show us many aspects of this problem. The person who knows nothing about baseball does not care who wins or loses, and is only interested in the spectacle. Such a person is relatively unattached. If such a person continues to watch baseball, soon he will learn enough about the techniques and rules of a baseball game that he will feel disappointed if something goes wrong in the game. Such a person has become more attached to the game and so is more affected by it. Eventually this person becomes a fan and has a favorite team. No longer is the game a pleasant spectacle, and the person loses the "take it or leave it" attitude. Now every play and every official's call become emotional issues because this person is completely attached to the baseball game. If his favorite team wins, he loves everyone; if his favorite team loses, he hates the team that won the game.

The more we are attached to something the greater the pain or pleasure will be. As we grow older we become attached to many different things and life becomes a confusing, frustrating mass of emotional stress. For children, matters seem very fundamental and simple. If a child sees an apple sitting on a table and he wants the apple, he will not think twice about grabbing the apple. On the contrary, an adult will begin to think twice or more times about taking the apple. He may think, "Whose apple is it? Should I eat it?" and so on. Things become much more confusing for adults because there are too many man-made thoughts that interfere with our real feelings. We are separated from the natural feelings we had as a child. We become confused because we are living these man-made values.

Different religions have particular laws to help an individual overcome his attachment to his body and ego, and sacrifice them to God. Some suggest that a person forget himself so that he can be open-minded and accepted by God. Other religions enforce a detachment from the body so that one can become free from all of the body's ramifications. All of these religious suggestions are sophisticated, too abstract for everyday people to live. These suggestions are far more easily said than done. They are much too difficult to follow unless we are prepared to live like a monk.

One way of knowing that it is not natural to become attached is by looking at the use of our hands. We may use the right hand more than the left hand, but we do not get angry at the left hand. If we would react the way we do in most circumstances, we would become mad at the left hand for having it so easy. But we know this is not true. We treat the right and left hands equally even if the right hand is used more. We feel a Yin-Yang balance and harmony between the right hand and left hand. So we can understand and learn from this that the attachment to all negative activities prevents us from knowing ourselves, and it is the lack of self-knowledge that allows this continual self-destruction. This paradox must be resolved if we are to understand ourselves as we understand our right and left hands.

If we try to operate a very complex, sensitive, and fragile machine without a thorough understanding of how it operates, we will probably destroy it by mistake. The operating manual, the language in which it is written, and the original intent and purpose behind the construction of this machine is its Yin aspect. If we can find the Yin aspect of this machine, then we can understand it, begin to operate it for its intended purpose without destroying it, and eventually maybe even enlarge upon its use.

You yourself are such a machine, both delicate and fragile. You cannot hope to operate your own machine without discovering the Yin aspect. If you can be aware of your "operating manual", you can then develop your true self and talent to a maximum. Then you can do something good for yourself and for others.

If we don't know our own Yin aspect, then we will live a confused, self-destructive, and generally unhealthy life. We see the results of this lack of information everyday. One person has natural talent for mathematics, but spends his whole life studying English. Another person's musical talent is never developed because everyone is pushing him to become a dentist. The unhappy, frustrated, and unful-filled lives of the majority of people are all the result of the lack of knowledge of their Yin aspect. It is apparent, then, that methods of finding this Yin aspect, this "operating manual for the self", are absolutely necessary for fulfillment. Of course, the most effective method of searching for and finding this Yin aspect is through meditation. The specifics and techniques of this search will occupy a later chapter.

第 二 章

四 度 空 間

Fourth Dimension

2-1 The dimensions

The seventeenth century French philosopher and mathematician. René Descartes, habitually spent his mornings philosophizing while still in bed. During one of these speculations it occurred to him that the location of the tip of his nose in his bedroom could be specified by three arbitrary numbers: a, b, and c. The number *a* represented the distance of his nose tip from the outside wall beyond the end of the bed: *b*, its distance from the left side wall: and *c*, its elevation above the floor as shown in the figure 2-1a

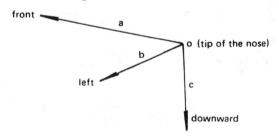

Figure 2-1a

While contemplating this association between a referenced location and a triplet of numbers, it became clear to him that any point in
the room could similarly be specified. His thought, though it seems
simple today, has been a major stepping-stone for modern civilization
because it created a way for man to relate numbers, equations, and
figures. Each of the numbers or coordinates, represented a distance or
length. It is to be noted that the number corresponding to a distance
is the ratio of its measure to that of a previously selected unit length.
Once a unit is established, it can be used to obtain the length of a line,
even if it is not straight. This then is called one-dimensional, the unit
length being sufficient to obtain the measure of magnitude.

Now consider an area in the plane, say the area of the bed in
Descarte's room projected on to the floor. We recognize intuitively
that the measure of length must now be used in another way.
Perimeter can be measured, but a new kind of unit is needed to
determine the area. Here the unit is used in two mutually perpendicular directions in the combination of cross product. The new unit, in
the shape of a square, may be duplicated a particular number of times
to cover the desired area in order to obtain its measure. The unit
square, while it contains the unit distance, is also completely beyond
the linear scope. An area may have any number of linear projections,
as shown in figure 2-1b:

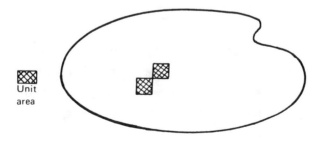

Unit
area

Figure 2-1b

Each linear projection relates to some aspect of the area, but none
of them, either simply or in combination, is sufficient to correctly

describe the two-dimensional figure. This fact gives the idea of dimension its significance. The analogy can be extended from the two-dimensional plane to the three dimensions of Cartesian space involving the separate dimensions of distance, length, width and height. Since we live in a three-dimensional world and is affected by the influence of time, which is considered the fourth dimension, we can understand the perspective of time as unchanging only in part and by analogy.

Now, let us discuss briefly the concept of dimension in geometry. A line has only one dimension, length; and a plane has two dimensions, length and width. On the next higher level a solid has three dimensions, length, width, and height.

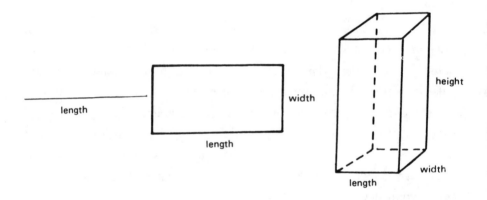

Figure 2-1c

We ordinarily experience space in terms of these three dimensions. Consider a drinking glass. We are familiar with this three-dimensional object through the combined sensations of sight and touch so we are easily able to produce an image of the combined experiences and know the shape and size of the drinking glass.

Things or objects in the two dimensional world have no thickness. If they had any thickness at all, like the film of silver on a mirror, they would be three-dimensional. Two examples of truly two-dimensional objects that we are familiar with are shadows and reflected images such as in a mirror. The general characteristics of two-dimensional objects are as follows:

1. There must generally be a three-dimensional object to either cast a shadow or reflect an image.

2. There must be a source of light to allow the shadow to be cast or the image reflected.

3. There must be something to receive the two-dimensional objects, such as a wall to the shadow, a polished surface to the image.

Therefore before a shadow or an image can be projected there must be three concurrent things; a three-dimensional object, light, and something to receive it.

Using the shadow as an example, we observe further characteristics of two-dimensional objects:

4. A shadow has no power to move by itself, which means its movement is objective, not subjective. A shadow moves only because either the light shines or the three-dimensional object moves or both move.

5. A shadow, since it has no thickness, can occupy the same area as another shadow. This cannot happen with three-dimensional objects. Once I sit in a chair, I must move away if someone else is to sit there.

6. A shadow may not have thickness, but its area can be limitless. A shadow grows in area as the light source and the three-dimensional object become closer together. However the plane upon which the shadow is cast stays stationary. This will continue until the three-dimensional object and the light source touch. If the three-dimensional object is able to cover up the light, the shadow will now be limitless on the other side of the object.

Generally, the shadow and the image have the same properties or characteristics. All the prior characteristics of shadows are also those of images with slight modifications. There are two differences between shadows and images which are very interesting. First, a shadow is a projection with the same orientation as the object that cast it, whereas the image is reversed in polarity from that which it reflects as shown in the figure 2-1d.

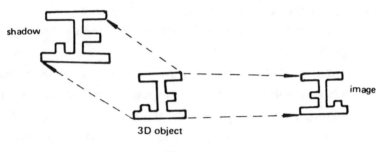

Figure 2-1d

Second, a shadow may be reflected as an image, but an image cannot cast a shadow as shown in the figure 2-1e.

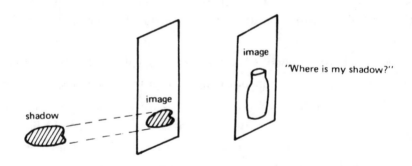

Figure 2-1e

Assume that a two-dimensional object, such as a shadow, has some sensation of its world. That object could sense only on the plane of length and width similar to our own but without a feeling of height. Imagine how a shadow might perceive a three-dimensional object such as a drinking glass. The plane where the shadow exists could be held in any of a number of relationships with the drinking glass; there might be no intersection, in which case no information is available, so the glass does not exist for the shadow, as shown in the figure 2-1f.

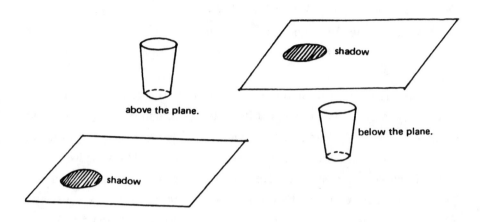

Figure 2-1f

The shadow's plane may touch the glass at one point or on one line segment. It might intersect the glass producing different cross-sections, such as a variety of sizes of circles, or, depending on the angle of the cross-section, an ellipse, a part of a parabola or hyperbola, or some other shape as shown in the figure 2-1g.

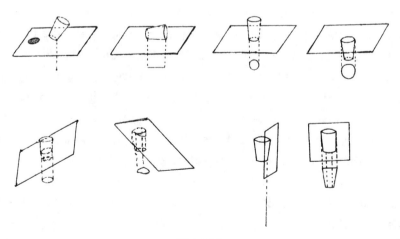

Figure 2-1g

Now here is the point. Each of these yield an authentic trace of the original — the drinking glass — yet no combination of these traces ever produces the fullness of the corresponding three-dimensional object.

There is a famous Indian story, "The Blind Men and the Elephant." A king summoned a number of blind men who had no idea of what an elephant was. The king asked them to stand in a circle around an elephant, each man touching a different part of it. Then the king said, "This is called an elephant. Now tell me what an elephant is like." The blind man who touched the side of the elephant said that an elephant was like a wall. The one who grasped the long trunk was frightened and said with a trembling voice, "Oh, no, it's like a giant snake." The blind man who examined the tail with his fingers said, "Not exactly, I would say an elephant is like a small snake, or rather a rope." Then the shortest man who was only able to hold the leg of the elephant said." My king, an elephent is just like the trunk of a tree."

The story depicts the situation of the shadow perceiving a three-dimensional object, but not completely. If the blind men would walk around the elephant, pay more attention and time, they would become aware of the total nature of the elephant, and know what it is like. The difference here is that the shadow lacks the sensation of height. The point, the line segment, different sizes of circles, a part of a parabola or a hyperbola, and so on, are all totally correct from a two-dimensional point of view. However, even if the shadow pays more attention and time, it will never get the entire picture of the drinking glass. The blind men, however, are capable of perceiving three-dimensional things, because they live in a three-dimensional world, even though they can't perceive the whole of a large object at once. The shadow will never understand the nature of the drinking glass because it exists in a two-dimensional world and lacks any idea or means to perceive the dimension of height.

The ideas and measurements of length and width will comprise the total body of the shadow's "scientific knowledge." The only way for the shadow to appreciate the drinking glass in its entirety is for the shadow to transcend the limitations of two-dimensional thinking.

Human beings have the same problem as the shadow. Like the shadow, which cannot perceive something above or below its plane, we live in a three-dimensional world, able only to experience reality in segments of time. No one knows what will happen in the future. No one can call the time back to repeat the past. We only perceive in the present. From the starting point, our birth, to the end point, our death, the continuity of life is perceived in slices, like the cross-sections of the drinking glass passing through the shadow. What is to us the present, is just one of countless cross-sections of the four-dimensional object.

What is the shape of life from a four-dimensional point of view? Is it like a drinking glass? Who can tell us? Would it be like our telling the shape of the drinking glass to the shadow? Suppose there are sentient beings who have a natural capacity to see the four-dimensional shape of things. To them time would be just another dimension and what we see as a drinking glass, would be to them the whole trace of the glass' existence? They could tell us what the shape of our life is; that is, they could see all at once what to us is separated as past, present and future. In a sense then, such beings would be as gods to us, just as we would be as gods to a shadow or a being of the two-dimensional world. A shadow has no motion without us and is instigated by our actions. Are we three-dimensional beings the shadows of four-dimensional beings? Since we are in the three-dimensional world that creates its world of shadow, we can create and control shadows and tell them about everything in their world. We could then define God as a being who is one dimension beyond that which we have been able to enter.

Man's epistemologies and methodologies are all right from a three-dimensional point of view, and since this is our only possible viewpoint, they constitute the best means to the truth about our reality. Every religion, philosophy, or science is right in three dimensions, just as the shadow's various perceptions of the drinking glass are all right from a two-dimensional point of view. The only way the shadow can see the whole drinking glass is to put all the parallel slices from the bottom to the top all together, and extrapolate the third dimension from the first two, as shown in the figure 2-1h.

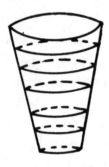

Figure 2-1h

But even with all the cross-sections of the glass arranged together, the shadow must still have enlightenment to perceive the third dimension — height. Otherwise, it will never truly understand it. It is as impossible for us to see the wholeness of time in "one moment", as it is for the shadow to see height in terms of width and length.

Man is the ruler in three dimensions, but he is the pawn of time. He has no control over it and no ordinary means of comprehending it as a dimension. Man is born and dies in time, and in between he only perceives the now-present, now-present, now-present of it. When he is twenty he can't see himself at sixty. When he is sixty, the young man of twenty is gone. He admonishes, "Know thyself," and forgets himself from minute to minute, unable to see the ends of his words or actions, or the beginning of the chain in which he is linked.

Our world to us is like the drinking glass to the shadow, we slice it here and get genetics, cut it from another angle and get chemistry, from another mathematics, from others psychology, history, etc. These are true pictures of three-dimensional reality. We slice it in many ways, and often, individuals will claim that their way is best. But we should keep in mind that because we are all describing a four-dimensional reality in terms of three-dimensions, this or that angle will never yield any absolute truth, just different equally valid slices of a "drinking glass." In this light, the jealousy, envy, bitterness, partisanship and criticism between human beings is sad and senseless. Some musicians snub their noses at pop music, some scientists maintain intense personal rivalries. Maybe his circular slice is bigger than mine, but his circle, my circle, you, me, we are all cross-sections; none better or worse, just different.

If people began to think past the limitations of three-dimensions, there would be more respect between men in the business of living together for the common good. Three-dimensional surface tensions would dissolve, and a spirit of cooperation and mutual generosity would spring up in human affairs.

⊘ 2-2 What is time?

Driving west across the middle of America the highway sometimes seems to extend endlessly in front of us. We have the feeling that our route is long and narrow. Miles ahead the sides of the road seem to converge and there is a point at which the distance is so great that, even on the clearest day the road disappears. When we stand at the edge of the ocean we get a sensation of immense width and breadth. The water stretches at all points before us to the edge of sky. If we sail out until the land is no longer visible we feel isolated, in the middle of an empty circle that encompasses us completely. We feel as if we were at the bottom of an inverted bowl of air and at the top of a vast bowl of water. If we look up from the bottom of the Empire State Building, we feel dizzy as our senses attempt to measure the height of the structure; the cars and pedestrians around us seem to fill up our senses and demand our attention. Yet from the building observation deck, the same height is experienced in reverse, and from that perspective, the cars and buses look like matchbox toys and the people are as tiny as insects.

Overwhelming as these impressions of immensity and distance seem to us, the effect is simply the result of the impact of three dimensions on our essentially short-sighted sense of perspective. But what about time? Can we see it as if it were a road stretching ahead of us? Can we hear it? Can we feel it as if it were spread around us like the waves of the ocean? Can we experience it as if from a great depth or a great height? Is it close to us or far away? We cannot see, nor feel, nor hear, nor sense time in any way. We cannot even imagine it. We say "time passes", but it doesn't fan our cheeks or ruffle our hair like the wind. And, though we can experience a sense of "looking back" or "looking forward" to things, the distance is intangible. There is no specific direction we can face in order to see the past, nor can we then turn around and see the future. No, while other things have a direct impact on us, time is indirect and subtle.

We think that we can make time, save time, spend time, waste time, as if it had substance, like money. Our first grasp of it came when we noticed that the sun rose and set regularly. This rhythmic pattern inspired us to try to measure the length of time between these occurrences, as if time had dimension. A sundial first permitted us to divide sunny days into hours. The hourglass or evenly burning candle enabled us to subdivide the hours into minutes. Mechanisms of increasing sophistication, weight and balance, pulley and pendulum, spring-tension, and electronic circuity, have helped to measure with increasing accuracy what we call time. But the clocks are merely calibrated against themselves, and against rhythmic processes of change in the observable universe. These mechanisms reinforce our three-dimensional sensation of time in which we state there are three kinds of time: the past, the present and the future. But the past only exists for us because we share a common biological organism that perceives and retains impressions of three-dimensional events. You may say, "Yes, but an hour ago you saw me eating breakfast." And I may have, but that event only exists for us because we see things in a similar way, and remember them similarly. As for the present, as soon as we say "present," it is past. The present really doesn't exist. However, paradoxically, we live in an abstract continuing present. As for the future, it is only a figment of our imagination.

In the naturally occurring universe, there is no past, present or future. All time exists simultaneously, just as points on a line exist simultaneously. A straight line of infinite length has no starting point, no end point. Man, however, so as to be able to relate this line to his own existence will call one point an origin and then call one direction from this point negative and the other direction positive as shown in the figure 2-2a.

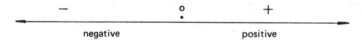

Figure 2-2a

This, however, is man-made, not natural. So it is with time. Just as a person can't relate to such a thing as a line with infinite length, one can't perceive time as a complete existence. We call a point on the line of time "present", just like the origin point. By defining one position of time as present, we then call one direction past (−) and the other direction future (+). This is all man-made and does not really exist.

From our point of view, an infinite line is too abstract to us, and only a line segment can be apprehended. So it is with our perception of time since our own life is like a very short segment of an infinite line. We are born at one point and die at another, defining a short measure of this infinite line, as shown in figure 2-2b

One's lifetime

Figure 2-2b

Between these two points we traverse this line segment beginning with all future at birth and ending with all past at death. Yet this short finite distance coexists with many other finite distances, all on this infinite line. Some of these are longer and some shorter. So it is with lifetimes. They coexist, some shorter, some longer. What is past for one lifetime is present for another and future for another, yet all coexist. Some ancient Chinese philosophers found this truth and stated that it seemed to make much ado about nothing.

What would be the fourth dimensional view of time? We can't talk about that because we have no way of knowing anything about it. It is beyond all three dimensional knowledge; it is a part of the Tao. Whatever we might say would be pure superstition or fiction. But we can imagine what our world of three dimensions might look like to a two-dimensional being such as a shadow which has no way of knowing about height. Then, by analogy, we might arrive eventually at some insight regarding our own relationship to a fourth dimensional reality. This is logical and there is no need to believe or not believe anything that cannot be agreed on.

A shadow has no perception of height as we do. So we can try to design experiments that might help to give a shadow the experience of height. For example, one plane might be placed perpendicular to a horizontal plane and the shadow can be moved along the horizontal plane until it arrives at the angle where the shadow will then gradually move up onto the vertical plane, and one side will be ascending while the other is still moving horizontally toward the vertical plane as shown in the figure 2-2c.

 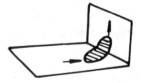

Figure 2-2c

Or again, we might hold a sheet between two people and cause a shadow to be cast on the middle of it. Then the two people can ruffle the sheet, moving it up and down in waves so the shadow seems to ripple as shown in the figure 2-2d.

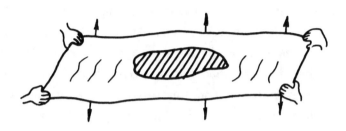

Figure 2-2d

This is similar to the ripple effect of the shadow of an airplane as it passes over the buildings in a city, moving up and down, and being cast partially on one building and partially on another behind it. Another example is the uneven shadow cast on a field by a bird in flight.

Can someone design an experiment to give three-dimensional beings the sensation of time? The answer is definitely yes! Two Chinese stories about time will illustrate this. The first story is called "The Governor of Nanku" (南柯太守傳) by Lee, Kung-tsu (李公佐 770 – 850 A.D.)

A man named Mr. Chun (淳于棼) lived 10 miles east of the town of Kuang-Ling (廣陵). South of his house stood a big locust tree. On the 7th of September in the ninth year of Chen-Kuan (貞觀 629-649 A.D.) Mr. Chun drank so much that he felt sick, and his two friends had to bring him home. He lay down on a bench on the east porch of his house, while one of his friends took care of his horse, and his other friend washed his own feet which were muddy from the ride. Mr. Chun fell asleep and in his dream he saw two messengers in purple clothes who had come from court to say that the king wished to see him. He stepped out of his house and saw a beautiful carriage waiting for him. He got in and the two messengers drove the carriage toward the big locust tree south of his home. They entered a large hole in the trunk of the tree and inside, Mr. Chun saw a lovely farmland with green fields, houses and villages. Finally, they came to a great city and passed under the gate. Over the arch, Mr. Chun saw characters inscribed in gold which said, "The Kingdom of the Great Locust Tree." They came at last to the palace where he became a valuable adviser to the king who had heard about Chun's many talents and appreciated him more and more each day. The king grew so fond of Mr. Chun that he gave him his daughter, the princess, in marriage and appointed him Minister of Nan-Ku (南柯太守). Mr. Chun held this post for thirty years, administering the government so wisely and well, that culture thrived under his influence and the people enjoyed unparalleled prosperity. A shrine was built in his honor by the grateful populace and a monument was erected on which was inscribed the record of his administration. The king recalled him to court and gave him a high office among his counselors. By his wife, the princess, he had five sons and two daughters, and was very content. However, the neighboring kingdom of The Vine or Tan-Lo attacked the kingdom of the Great Locust Tree, and Mr. Chun was made general of the army. But Mr. Chun lost the first great battle and, at the same time, in the palace, Mr. Chun's wife died. The king removed Mr. Chun from office, and appointed another general. Even in retirement, Mr. Chun retained his dignity and power, and the people looked up to him. The king became suspicious and was afraid of his influence among the people. So the king forbade him to be seen by the people, confined him to his house, and placed guards around it. Finally, the king decided to return him to his former village and his humble status. As the soldiers took him away, Mr. Chun thought sadly about his long life, rich in service and honor, and blessed with joy. He remembered his wife, his children and his many friends. Suddenly, he opened his eyes and found himself lying on the bench on the east porch of his house. He looked around and saw his boy-servant sweeping the yard, his one friend still washing his feet, and the other still currying the horse. The golden rays of the setting sun still shone on the garden wall, and a cup of tea that had been set beside him was still warm. In the few minutes he had been asleep, Mr. Chun lived an entire life-time.

Here is another Chinese story about time called Lan-Ko San (爛柯山) or Rotten Ax-shaft Mountain, a mountain located in the southeastern province of Chekiang, in the district Chu-Chou. The scenery is wild and beautiful. The cliffs are rugged and sheer, as in the landscapes of the southern painters. In the yellow light of early morning a woodcutter set out into these mountains, carrying his ax over his shoulder. He whistled happily as he strode along. After a while he came to a high place where he saw two old people seated upon rocks on either side of a massive rock which, they were using as a table to play Go, a Chinese board game. One was dressed in red and the other in black. The woodcutter was a great fan of Go, and so he paused to watch. The opponents didn't say a word and kept their eyes on the board. Even under normal circumstances the game of Go takes a long time, and is deeply fascinating to those who can follow its strategies. These two players seemed to be of equal strength and were engaged in very subtle and complex play. The woodcutter soon grew so absorbed that he laid his ax down and sat upon it so as to be more comfortable. The two old people passed a peach slowly back and forth between them, from which first one and then the other would take a bite. The woodcutter realized how hungry he was and wished that they would offer him some. But the two finished the peach and tossed the pit to the ground. The woodcutter noticed that some of the fruit still clung to the pit and he picked it up and sucked on it. The game ended at last and the players collected the pieces, folded the board and went away. The woodcutter stood up, stretched his legs and reached for his ax. But when he picked the ax up the rusty head fell away from the handle and the handle crumbled into rotten fragments in his hand. This surprised the woodcutter greatly for he always kept the blade sharp and shiny, and the handle had been strong, well-seasoned wood. The sun told the woodcutter it was not quite noon as he hurried down the mountain to his village. When he got there, he looked around in even greater surprise, for nothing was familiar to him. Everything had changed. On the spot where his little hut had been stood a much larger house. He knocked and a young woman opened the door. He didn't recognize her, nor she him. He asked her about the village he had known, but though her last name was the same as his, she could not answer any of his questions. Among her family and her neighbors, none could answer his questions. Finally, her grandfather brought out the records of the family and discovered that one of their ancestors had been a wood-cutter who had never returned from the mountains one morning, three hundred years ago.

For us, these two stories are analagous to the tests which we designed for the shadow. In those tests, we tried to imagine how it might be possible to give a two-dimensional being the sensation of height. In the story of Mr. Chun, we see that a man, in his dream, is able to fully experience a great span of past, present, and future in only a few moments of ordinary time. He lives a normal lifetime in the space of a few minutes. How different will be his view of time from then on? In the story of the woodcutter, we are told of a man who experiences the passage of only a few hours while in the company of two fourth-dimensional beings. When they leave and he returns to human society, he discovers, like Washington Irving's Rip Van Winkle, that 300 years have gone by. The bewildered woodcutter surely lives in a new world after experiencing the dimension of time.

Another Chinese story sheds light on our attempts to describe time in terms of space and speed, on the calibrations of the clock, or through the cyclical processes of observable nature. It begins on a warm morning in the springtime, at the edge of a still, green pond. In the shallows a large number of tadpoles are swimming. From the muddy bank, a full-grown spotted frog jumps into the pond amongst the tadpoles. They gather around her with many questions. "Tell us,

Mother, what you have seen of the world beyond the water!" "Yes, tell us what it is like!" They listen eagerly as she speaks. "The world is warm and very bright," she says. "There is a great yellow fire called the Sun, high in a blue sky. It is nice to sit in the mud of the bank and feel the heat of the Sun on my back. A breeze blows to me across the fields that surround this pond and ruffle the surface of the water. Flowers of many colors wave over me, and I can smell their sweet fragrance mingled with the smell of earth and green willow trees. Through the air, the hum of bees comes to me along with the dry sounds of dragonfly wings. Yes, my children, it is a wide world, very full and beautiful and comfortable, and all of it seems to be stretching and growing as I am in the sunlight." "What is the sunlight, Mother?" the tadpoles ask. "What is wind?" "What are flowers?" "What is smell?" "How do you smell earth or hear the wings of the dragonflies?" Their questions were endless, and they all spoke at once, clamoring for answers. Their mother became irritated and said, "I will not answer any more questions, you are all too young to understand. Some day when you drop your tails, maybe you will know what I am talking about." Sure enough, a little later that season, the first of the tadpoles outgrew his tail, left the water and stepped out into the air of late Spring. The Sun was warm and the many-colored flowers nodded in a light breeze. The young frog sat on the bank and drank in the sensations of the world of air. He did not have to be told.

We who philosophize about time, we who are limited to three dimensions are like a school of tadpoles wondering about another world. Until we too are able to "drop our tails" and step into that dimension, time must remain a subject of speculation for us, as a drinking glass is to a shadow. Until we can experience time as a dimensional context, it must remain a flat reflection to us as the upper world is to the water-bound tadpole.

The world of the shadow is totally comprehensive to us because we can see at once what is above and below its plane. The shadow, however, can only speculate about what are to it the non-tangible

concepts of "space above" and "space below." Though we might see
its world as very limited and feel superior to it, we ourselves exist in
a narrow plane which we call the present, and to us the concepts of
"time past" and "time-future" are equally intangible. It is very easy
for us to transcend the limitations of two dimensions. We define
"above" and "below" in terms of a frame of reference such as the table
top on which the shadow lives. If we remove the table top, "above"
and "below" as the shadow conceptualized them are easily seen as one
space to us. We encounter greater difficulty when we try to remove the
"table top" of the present. A fourth dimensional being, however,
would be able to remove the limitation of the "present" in perception
of time as easily as we can disregard the table top in our perception of
space. We can no more move forward and backward in time than the
shadow can move up or down at will in space. We know that the
shadow is cast three-dimensionally in space, but the shadow only
perceives its existence on the two-dimensional plane such as the table
top that intercepts its three-dimensional form. Perhaps we are shadows
cast in four dimensions and only perceive our existence when it is
intercepted by a three-dimensional construct, such as "the present."
The shadow would look on us as gods if it could see that we are not
limited in our movements through a space which to it is purely
theoretical. How would we view beings who could view all time as if it
were "present," and act in the past or future at will?

We can eat off the top of the table where the shadow lives and
stretch our legs out underneath it. However, we have to wait till
the hour at which the time lock on our bank vault is set in order to
withdraw money, we must set aside half an hour to drive thirty miles.
A being living in four dimensions would not have to wait to withdraw
money: For him, the vault is not closed, but open as it was yesterday
morning and will be tomorrow morning. He can have money whenever
he wishes. If he wishes to travel thirty miles, he does not have to drive.
He can be there instantly. For him, time is no barrier, but an open
world, just as for us the shadow's hypothetical "above" and "below" is

the space in which we live.

 ## 2-3 Where can we find the truth?

In *The Equality of All Things,* Chuang-Tzu, the great Chinese Taoist philosopher and a contemporary of Mencius (372-289 B.C.), wrote:

> "Once I, Chuang-Tzu, dreamed I was a butterfly. I enjoyed my life, flying happily here and there, having forgotten who I was, believing myself to be a butterfly. Suddenly, I woke up and I was Chuang-Tzu again. Did Chuang-Tzu dream he was a butterfly, or is the butterfly now dreaming he is Chuang-Tzu? Is there any difference between the two? It is the way of change to make one thing into another, and all things are equal."

In his dream, Chuang-Tzu's consciousness became that of a butterfly. He perceived the world as if he were a butterfly, and as far as he knew during that time, he was a butterfly indeed. Then when he awoke, he wondered whether the butterfly was dreaming he was Chuang-Tzu. However, an onlooker would not have noticed any transformation, but would only have seen Chuang-Tzu's body sleeping and then waking up.

An unchanging principle underlying changing things is present throughout nature. Water in warm sunshine is vaporized and drawn up into the sky as clouds. There are an infinite number of cloud types and formations, which occur under varying conditions. At a certain point the water will precipitate back to earth as rain, or if the temperature is low enough, as sleet, hail or snow. In winter, the surface of lakes and rivers freezes into ice. Throughout these changes of state, the molecular formula H_2O remains the same.

In this common example of constancy in change, perhaps we can learn a little about the changes which seem to affect our lives more intimately, such as the processes of birth and death. From the waters' point of view, when it begins to freeze to ice, it is dying as water and being born as ice. From the ice's point of view, as it melts, it dies as a solid and is born as a liquid. However, if we take the point of view of

H_2O, whether water freezes into ice or ice melts into water there is neither birth nor death. They are both H_2O. When a baby is born, we feel quiet joy and congratulate the mother and father. When a man dies, we feel quiet sorrow and sympathy for his wife and family. From Nature's point of view, there is no joy at birth or sorrow at death. Why is this? Because our body is actually a combination of approximately 65% water, more than 10% minerals, and about 10% various kinds of hydrocarbons and other elements. To Nature, as onlooker, it doesn't matter that dust walks around a while as a man, nor does anything increase or decrease in nature when the water, minerals, and other elements that make up a human body return to earth and re-form as something else. Our birth and death are just other transformations of one form to another. Do we feel joy or sorrow when water changes to ice or ice to vapor?

Buddhists always admonish their believers to understand "birth is death, death is birth," "everything visible is empty," and "the immaterial is the material." Taoists use a more scientific method to abstract these concepts, and use the expression "Yin is Yang, Yang is Yin." Chuang-Tzu discussed this paradox in relation to the ideas of right and wrong:

> "Suppose you and I argue
> and you win.
> Are you right and am I wrong?
> If I had won,
> Would I have been right and you wrong?
> Are we both partly right and partly wrong?
> Are we both all right and all wrong?
> If you and I cannot see the truth,
> Whom shall I ask to be the judge?
> Shall I ask someone who agrees with you?
> If he already agrees with you can he be a fair judge?
> Shall I ask someone who agrees with me?
> If he already agrees with me can he be a fair judge?
> Shall I ask someone who disagrees with both of us?
> If he already disagrees with both of us can he be a fair judge?
> Shall I ask someone who agrees with both of us?

If he already agrees with both of us, can he be a fair judge?
If you and I and others cannot decide,
Where shall we find a judge?
Waiting for changing opinions is waiting for nothing.
Seeing everything in relation to the heavenly cosmos
And leaving the different viewpoints as they are
We may be able to live out our years.
What do I mean
By seeing things in relation to the heavenly cosmos?
Consider right and wrong, being and non-being.
If right is indeed right,
There need be no argument
About how it is different from non-being.
Forget time, forget distinction.
Enjoy the infinite; rest in it.

Chuang-Tzu understood and expressed the paradox of the identity of opposites. He used philosophy as a means of reaching the people of his time and culture with that message. Philosophy, poetry, and other intuitive, holistic ways of viewing the world have always been close to the mainstream of the Chinese world view and civilization. Although these have also been important in the West, the individual person in Western society has historically had a more practical, scientific and analytical perspective. In recent generations, we in the West have lived in the context of an increasingly technological culture, in which it is more and more difficult for any one man to achieve an overview or comprehend the total picture. For someone to reconstruct a telephone or a television, for example, he must undergo sophisticated training, and he would consequently have less energy to invest in his business or his study. A professional who wishes to keep up with rapidly advancing knowledge and techniques must sacrifice time he might have used to broaden his understanding of the other aspects of his life. The engineer may not be able to spend much time with literature. The sociologist may have neither time nor inclination to study physics. The biologist may know very little about history or philosophy. All of these are equally valid ways of perceiving the

world. Unfortunately, this increasing need for specialization, in sports
and in leisuré pastimes as well as in business, can isolate every man from
his neighbor, if he becomes convinced of the "rightness" of his
viewpoint and the comparative ignorance of other men.

If society were a building, it is as if every person was looking out
of a different window and each feels his view to be the best. The same
is the case with knowledge. Eastern philosophy is a window and
Western science is another window. Maybe we can say every viewpoint
is right. We can also say that each viewpoint is only partial, and
therefore partly not right. Yet both viewpoints exist in the same
building, within the system whose construction is based on our senses.

As a concrete example of the paradox of perspective, consider
the wife who weeps at the death of her husband. A passerby may feel
sympathy for her but feel no personal sense of grief at the deceased
man's death. The wife is part of the system which has changed as a
result of her husband's death, but the passerby lives outside the man's
system. For him, there is no change at all. So the point of view of
these two individuals is totally different. This is the paradox of the
complete picture, and can be illustrated by a further concrete example.

Let two individuals be represented by the points A and B, the
sense of right and wrong by the means of front and behind. We now
ask these two individuals which one is in front and which one is behind,
just like Chuang-Tzu's question of who is right and who is wrong. This
question cannot be answered, however, without information about the
system in which A and B exist, as shown in the figure 2-3a.

.   .

A   B

Figure 2-3a

Suppose, then, we represent the system by a line connecting A and
B, as shown in the figure 2-3b.

Figure 2-3b

Again we ask who is in front and who is behind. We still, however, are unable to answer the question, because while A and B are connected in the system defined by the straight line, we lack a standard reference or perspective from which to make a comparison. Now in the figure below, we connect A and B with a line marked with a directional arrow as shown in figures 2-3c. and 2-3d.

Figure 2-3c   Figure 2-3d

In the Figure 2-3c we can easily state that B is in front of A; in the figure 2-3d A is in front of B.

But suppose we redefine the system containing A and B as a circle as shown in the figure 2-3e.

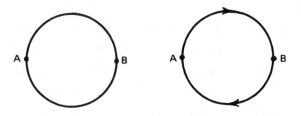

Figure 2-3e

Once again it is impossible to determine who is in front. In the linear system, this difficulty was resolved by assigning a direction to the line connecting A and B. In the figure above right, then, let us define a direction to the circle. This time, however, we have a paradox. As we move along the circle for a while, B appears to be in front and A behind. But as we continue along the circle, it appears that A is in front and B behind. In this system there is no absolute answer to the question of who is in front.

This paradox of the circle brings us back to the Taoist philosophy that Yin is Yang and Yang is Yin. While this way of thinking permeates Eastern philosophy, art, and activities including T'ai Chi and meditation, it is a difficult concept to grasp from the perspective of other systems. To illustrate this point, let us consider the relationship between East and West in the plane as shown in the figure 2-3f.

West  East

Figure 2-3f

Given any two points on a plane, it is always possible to determine which is East of the other. As we move between two points anywhere in this system, we can always say unambiguously whether we are moving from East to West or from West to East, so there is no paradox no question about what is true.

If instead of a plane, however, we define the system as a sphere; or the surface of the terrestrial globe, East and West are no longer absolute. Because the hemispheres are formed by cutting a globe in half along the Prime Meridian which runs from pole to pole through Greenwich, England. It is the starting place for measuring longitude or distances East and West in degrees. East and West longitude both run from zero degrees to 180 degrees where they meet as shown in figure 2-3g.

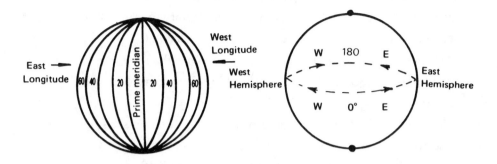

Figure 2-3g

As we move East along the equator or a latitude line from zero longitude to 180 degrees, the Eastern hemisphere suddenly ends and we enter the Western hemisphere. Thus East becomes West. As we continue in the same direction in the Western hemisphere, we eventually enter the Eastern hemisphere again. Now, West has become East. It seems, paradoxically, that the end of East is West, and the end of West is East. It is in this sense that the Taoists say that the extreme of Yin is Yang, and the extreme of Yang is Yin.

These coordinates, East and West, are man-made. Without the general agreement that zero degree longitude is at Greenwhich, perhaps every country would have chosen one of its own cities as the zero point. China might pick Peking, the United States might pick Wichita. Then there would be trouble and much confusion. The recognized standard simplifies human relations, but obscures the truth of the equal rightness of a multiple viewpoint. Because there are no directional absolutes, East and West are arbitrary designations; but the more men agree on the definition of East and West, the more the man-made things become natural standards.

In China, each year is represented by a different animal in a twelve year cycle. A Chinese story tells that in the beginning the animals got together to decide who would go first. The tiger, rabbit, dragon, snake, horse, sheep, monkey, rooster, dog, and pig were able to agree about the order of their appearance, one after another. But the ox and the mouse could not agree, and got into an argument. Neither would agree to let the other go first. Finally the ox said:

"I'll tell you why I should go first: I'm bigger than you are."

But the mouse said: "Oh no! I should go first, then, because I'm bigger!"

"You? You're bigger? If you can prove that then you may go first," said the ox. "But how could you prove so preposterous a thing?"

"We'll get people to judge which of us is bigger," said the mouse.

"Oh well then," said the ox, "it's obvious which of us is bigger. I'm sure to be first."

The mouse said, "We'll walk through the village, and if people say What a big ox! then you may go first. If they say what a big mouse! then I'll go first."

The ox agreed.

Now the ox was certainly a large, strong animal. But he was no bigger than any other ox. The mouse, however, was larger than any other mouse, and with his hair fluffed out, he was a very large mouse indeed. So when they walked through the village, the people ran out of their houses crying, "Look! What a big mouse! What a big mouse!" For they had seen many oxen of that size before, but they'd never seen so large a mouse. The mouse went first.

This story illustrates the relativity of truth. None would have said that the mouse was bigger than the ox, if actual size that were the only frame of reference. However, the villagers were not operating within the ox's frame of reference, but within a frame in which the ox was commonplace and the mouse was truly extraordinary.

If "small" and "big" replaced "east" and "west" in our previous diagrams, we see that the ox was thinking of size as a single isolated linear continuum, where he was nearer the pole of absolute bigness, and the mouse was closer to the pole of smallness as shown in the figure 2-3h.

Figure 2-3h

The mouse, though, was able to perceive that "big" can become "small" and "small" become "big", as in the circular or spherical continuum:

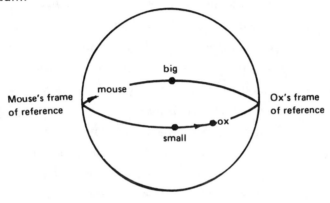

Figure 2-3i

In this system, the mouse may be "bigger" than the ox in a relative position as shown in figure 2-3i.

In our world, there are roughly opposing basic views, one of which sees the world from linear and flat perspectives, the other as a set of concentric and closure curves and spheres. We have surrounded ourselves with flat surfaces and straight edges: doors, tables, walls, etc. All reflect a two-dimensional orientation. Men even believed for a long time that the earth itself was flat. Analytical thinking, too, proceeds in a linear fashion, from premises to resolution. However, the context for this view, the earth and its natural phenomena, its orbit, its sister planets and their orbits, and space itself, exhibits varying degrees of roundness. Eastern philosophy and Western science have both accepted roundness and identity in natural systems. Western popular philosophy has not come so far. The Western mind still has a difficult time accepting that Yin can become Yang, and Yang can become Yin, or that Yin is Yang, and Yang is Yin.

While Western society still is reluctant to grant legitimacy to any but the linear functions of the mind, it is easy to see that emotions are circular. Happiness succeeds sadness, sadness follows happiness, elation preceeds depression, "pride comes before a fall." When joy reaches extremes, it is often followed by a period of neutral or negative feelings. Our bodies teach us this natural cycle. We sometimes laugh so hard we cry, and some situations are so hard to accept or so disappointing that there is nothing to do but laugh.

Our cumulative knowledge has emerged from both the linear and circular systems of thought, and application of the appropriate thought system results in a maintenance of balance. For example, viewing a transient emotional state such as depression as a permanent and unalterable reality tends in itself to perpetuate that state. Recognition of the circular nature of emotion, on the other hand, permits a clearer perspective regarding the existing emotional state and accelerates the transition away from that state. Moreover, the boundaries between these systems are often only vaguely defined and frequently can be removed to reveal a basic underlying unity which precludes all but a semantic distinction. When, for example, we drive from coast to coast across the country, we may think of the linear aspect of this travel in terms of mileage between end to end. However, at the same time, we are really moving along the surface of a sphere, the earth, and in doing so we are defining an arc. Even the path of a rocket to the moon was first thought of as a line, that being supposedly the shortest distance between two points. But it was discovered that the necessary trajectory is a curve that accounts for orbit, gravity, rotation and the relative motion of the two spheres.

Long ago people were bothered by the question of absolute origin. Even wise men, scientists, and philosophers spent much time debating simple questions, such as whether the egg or the chicken had come first. These dilemmas were the result of linear ways of thinking. When it was believed that the earth was flat, another question was whether day or night had come first. But the discovery that the earth was spherical showed that the whole system was circular and that the earth experienced day and night simultaneously. Day and night, within the whole system, are constantly changing into each other. So although "sequence" is an important consideration within a linear frame of reference, sequence ceases to have significance from the total, or circular point of view, where the chicken-egg distinction has no absolute beginning point.

Men debate the existence of reincarnation even today. Men who hold only the linear point of view find it is impossible to accept the idea that birth is anything but an absolute beginning, and death is anything but an absolute end. From a circular point of view, birth and death are simply stages in a continuum of life. They are the Yin and Yang aspects of the same event. From this perspective, reincarnation is a natural, self-evident process.

Men who think in linear terms believe that they may be able to escape the consequences of their actions. They think that if they are clever enough, they can get around the law, or do things that are wrong and benefit by them, as long as no one else finds out. It is difficult to convince men who hold this point of view, otherwise except by outward shows of force: public law, vigilant police and swift justice. Most of the religions, however, accepting the circular concept teach an inevitable private morality. People who realize that everything is circular accept the idea that every action will have its automatic reaction, and that there is no way to be the "cause" without receiving the "effect". The agent of cause will be repaid as the cycle of effect returns to him or his family. Good acts will eventually benefit him, and harmful acts will certainly harm him.

We have used the circular model to investigate more complex ideas than we could with the linear. We might also go on to look at ellipsoid, parabolic, hyperbolic, helical or other models. But even then, the situation is as previously mentioned. All these systems are only different windows of the same building. We would have come only to the edges of three-dimensional knowledge. The truth still eludes us.

To discover the truth about the circulating of causality, and the chicken and egg question, we must go outside the "building" to comprehend the whole picture; we must see three dimensions in the light of the fourth dimension: time.

The chicken and the egg problem is similar to the minting of a coin.   Did the head side come first, or the tail side?   Neither, they were both struck at the same time. Heads and tails are equal aspects of the same coin.   So the chicken and the egg are simply aspects of fourth dimensional reality.   In time, they are the same.   In space, if there is a plane of reference such as a sheet of paper or a table top, then there is a sense of "above" and "below".   If the sheet or the table top is taken away, however, there is no sense of above and below; it is all the same space.   In our three-dimensional causal world, we have beginnings and endings because of our partial sense of time.   But if that limited reference is removed, there is no beginning and no end.   Beginnings and endings become part of one time.   In the fourth dimension all time can be experienced simultaneously, without present, past, and future; without a start or a conclusion.

Anything we agree about in our three-dimensional world, any observations we make, are the effects of causes beyond our perception in the fourth dimension. We can see this by observing that the two-dimensional world of a shadow is created by three dimensional phenomena.   The shadow of a car in motion can study and research its existence only so far.   It can discover that it is moving.   It can measure its area.   But it has no way of knowing when it will stop moving or where it is coming from or going to, or why it changes shape periodically (as the car turns at different angles to the sun).   In the three dimensional world, we can observe weather, for example, and predict it with fair accuracy for a week or so in advance, but we don't know the long range reasons for the changes.   To us, they appear random.   Our powers of prediction allow us to discover patterns, but not to account for infinite variation.   Why do "good men" sometimes die young?   Why do very bad people sometimes have a long, good life?

We can take averages, study statistical probability, and plot life expectancy, but we are unable to see that later this afternoon this person will be run over by a bus, or next year that person will invent a better mousetrap. Like the shadow, we are only able to study the characteristics of our own dimension; the "why" of them, the *cause,* of which we are the *effect,* is the car. We are just its shadow.

After many pages of discussion, it is still no easier to describe the ability to sense the fourth dimension that comes in T'ai Chi Chuan and meditation. Similarly, we would have great difficulty attempting to accurately describe the taste of an apple to someone who had never eaten one. It is beyond the power of words to provide the direct experience of the things they symbolize. We are talking here about an understanding which can only be experienced individually in action and which cannot be passively acquired by reading. Language is based heavily on the perception of the eyes. These things, however, are sensed *within* the body, beyond the power of the eyes to see, or the ears to hear. The purpose of T'ai Chi Chuan is to seek stillness in motion. The aim of meditation is to seek action in inaction. This is experienced from the sense of their opposites within motion and within tranquility. It is possible with patience and persistence to feel, as if intuitively, very subtly, very delicately, the nature of time. By following this feeling we may move close enough to the border of the fourth dimensional world to get a glimpse of that reality. This is the first stage of enlightenment.

第 三 章

靜坐的哲學基礎

Philosophy

☯ 3-1 The Goal of Meditation

There are various explanations which can be offered to the question "why meditate?" Undoubtedly, no one explanation will satisfy everyone. Just as the shadow is able to intersect the same drinking glass from many different angles, so each individual will approach meditation from a different point of view. The following analogy may be offered to make the most complete picture of a reason for meditation.

Meditation can be explained in terms of education. Like education, meditation is a practice on a number of different levels for a variety of different purposes. For example, a wide range of programs are offered in adult schools for community education. Because the adult school administrators realize that community residents have many different needs and interests, they attempt to provide courses and activities of an academic, social, vocational, recreational, and practical nature. Clearly, the concept of education is a broad term which encompasses all of the various purposes.

Likewise, meditation is a broad term which includes a wide range of purposes. For example, meditation can be utilized as a relaxation exercise and may help anxious people relieve a variety of stress related illnesses. Meditation alone, or combined with breathing techniques or Chi-Kung, can be used as a form of therapy for the mind and body. In the East, there is a wealth of knowledge available through thousands of years of experience in healing illnesses such as insomnia, high blood pressure, influenzas, asthma, etc., through meditation. Meditation, however, is not just a form of how-to-cure yourself therapy. It can improve the ability to concentrate which can in turn enhance every aspect of daily life.

There are those individuals who have never heard of meditation or who would argue that they live perfectly at peace without the use of meditation. These people have concluded that since they are okay as they are, there is no need to start something as seemingly difficult as meditation. Those reluctant to take up meditation can be compared to illiterate individuals who would assert that they are quite satisfied without the benefits of educaton.

It might be true that an illiterate person could live on a beautiful island with a home standing in a garden and overlooking the sea. He might be wealthy with a large number of attendants. But the philosophical question still remains: Does he enjoy life as fully as possible? Perhaps inside this man lives a poet who would like to sing of the wind or toy with the moon. Due to his lack of education, however, he lives beyond the knowledge which could allow him to experience living the leisurely abandon of a poet. He cannot read or write, and therefore might not be experiencing his life to its' fullest enjoyment. Perhaps education could enhance this man's life in a way that he cannot yet realize.

The same is true of meditation. Our lives can be enhanced by it, but it is in a way that can only be experienced on a very personal level.

There is a more advanced aspect of meditation as well, which would be roughly equivalent to graduate training in terms of our educational system. In graduate school, we learn to concentrate on a particular area of study and to develop a certain way of thinking by following the methods considered appropriate for the chosen field, whether scientific, literary, historical, legal or philosophical. However, this training is just the beginning of our professional development. After graduate school is completed, we may not only teach or practice what has been learned, we may also begin to explore an idea through special advanced research. Similarly, as we progress through advanced meditation techniques, we learn to develop our thinking and then to explore our lives. What is found depends not only on the method and on chance, but on natural ability and devotion to practice.

Unfortunately, just as scientists may spend years in research without making a major discovery, some meditators may conscientiously work toward a higher stage of wisdom without ever reaching it. For this reason, some individuals would suggest that meditation is a foolish endeavor.

Let us reflect on the words and life of Albert Einstein to gain another perspective. He said: "If my theory of relativity proves correct, my associates will call me a genius, Americans will call me a friend, and Germans will call me a German. If my theory proves false, my associates will call me a fool, Americans will call me a German, and Germans will call me a Jew."

In this statement, we see that Einstein took the chance to invest his life into an endeavor whereby if he found an answer, he would greatly enhance human knowledge, receive just recognition, and find his equivalent to enlightenment. Truly, Einstein was an exceptional man, not only because he proved the theory of relativity, but because he took the chance of pursuing the goal of his enlightenment. The important point is that although we might not reach enlightenment through meditation, it is a grand enough aspiration for us to make the effort.

Although we have used education as an analogy to explain certain aspects of meditation, and to describe meditation in general, this analogy is limited. The approach, methods, and goals of each are totally different. Education proceeds by building or accumulating knowledge, step by step. A child who wants to write a composition must first learn the alphabet. Then, he must learn to write words. Eventually he will express himself in phrases, sentences, and finally will be able to write a short composition. However, this is just the beginning of the development of his writing ability, which he can continually improve as long as he lives. Sir Isaac Newton, near the end of his life, after his major contributions in the fields of mathematics and physics, said that he had merely found one shell on a vast seashore. Chuang-Tzu said that life has a limit, but knowledge is without limit, and when mortals pursue the unlimited, they must not expect to ever be able to comprehened it completely. Not only are our lives limited, but our senses, through which we perceive the world, are also limited, and easily distracted. Although we try to concentrate on a book or a paper, our absorption is never complete; our ears will stray to the music playing in another room, our eyes will leave the page, and our minds will think about tomorrow or yesterday. Our consciousness is a weak fist and cannot hold much of the immense amount of information we come into contact with in even our limited life. Education is always limited, though it yearns for completion.

Meditation offers another approach to the goal of a different quality of knowledge. If, for example, the shadow had completed its graduate work, it would at last be ready to do advanced research on drinking glasses. But its training would only have prepared it to conduct its investigations in two dimensions. No matter how long it lives, no matter how long it researches, no matter how smart it is, it will not describe the drinking glass satifactorily unless it is able to add the third dimension to its thinking. For the shadow, in a two dimensional world, perception of the third dimension results in enlightenment. In our three dimensional world, we are in the same fix. We will only attain enlightenment if we are able to perceive our reality from a fourth dimension.

In Chinese philosophy, progression to enlightenment occurs only as the practitioners are able to let go of prior attachments and ways of perceiving and doing. We can look to blind people as an example for inspiration at this point. Blind people learn to make their way through the world by developing their other senses to a much greater degree then people who can see would believe possible. Quite a few blind people have achieved greatness without having the use of their eyes. In fact, one particular well-known songwriter, Stevie Wonder, is famous for the use of imagery in his songs which create beautiful pictures in the minds of his listeners. Yet he has never seen the things he sings about, having been blind from birth. Such people are an inspiration in that they have used their imagination creatively to exceed their limitations. They are forced to do this if they are to succeed, because their handicaps place them in a situation of Wu Chi which others do not ordinarily experience.

To exceed our limitations, we must similarly experience Wu Chi and use our imagination creatively.

This emotional process of discarding what has been gained in order to perceive something new is representative of a deeper and more important process in Chinese philosophy. This is the constant cyclical process of going from Wu Chi to Tai Chi and back again. As each new stage of awareness, or higher consciousness, is developed, the practitioner has gone from Wu Chi to Tai Chi, But until the fixation upon this new level of perception is developed, the practitioners cannot be freed to move on to the next stage. When he is finally able to release himself from attachment to this level and attain a new and higher level of awareness, then this new prior level has become Wu Chi for him again. In comparison with the level he has now arrived at, the prior level with which he had been so fascinated has become meaningless· again. Although the stages are different, each in turn represents a movement from Wu Chi to Tai Chi and back to Wu Chi again.

There are many techniques which have been developed in order to enable us to experience increased self-knowledge through discarding prior attachments. In order to develop dexterity in the left hand, a right handed person would refrain from using the right hand. A further example is the three stages of Chinese boxing: The hand method, the torso method, and the mind method. The first refers to the hardened, external forms of boxing, where the emphasis is on hand strikes and kicks. These methods rely on the muscles to produce speed and the resulting force. In order to move to the torso method, the player learns to move the hands and feet by expressing his intention in his torso. The extremities then move only as the body expresses the essence of that movement to them. Here the techniques are used to develop total coordination and agility in body movement, and eventually the internal energy known as the Chi and the Chin. (See the Tao of Tai Chi Chuan by Jou, Tsung Hwa, 1981) In order to practice the mind method, the player shifts the emphasis inside, and neither the extremities nor the body act independenly, but follow the intention, which is complete in the mind, known as the "spirit" or Shen (神). The movement from stage to stage is accomplished by forgetting or shifting the emphasis from the hands to the body, then the body to the mind.

Another example of man's progression to greater degrees of achievement through the method of discarding prior techniques is in the development of speed. At first we used our legs to move as quickly as they would carry us. The wheel allowed us to forget our legs and travel much faster. When we deemphasized our legs and incorporated the use of the wheel on a bicycle, we could travel faster. But only by completely forgetting the legs and concentrating on the wheel alone could we attain a much greater speed than the bicycle — as we did by using a locomotive on a train with an engine in it powering the wheels. This was still not as fast as we could travel by forgetting about the wheel and developing wings to fly in airplanes. As long as the wheels are still used, however, the plane remains on the ground and speed is limited. Thus the prior method must be completed discarded, in order to attain still higher levels of achievement.

In similar fashion, we have gradually learned to forget our wings and concentrate on the jet, developing the rocket to enable us to travel at speeds previously unimaginable. But how can we travel faster than a rocket? To reach still greater levels of speed, we must continue to discard such devices. In the next stage, a satellite rotates around the earth at great speed without the use of jet propulsion. But the earth itself travels at an even more tremendous speed in spinning and rotating around the sun. Natural things can always exceed the limitations of those which are man-made. To travel even faster, we must give up tangible nature. Light, which is such an intangible substance, can travel between the sun and the earth in just seven minutes. We might ask how man may achieve such a velocity? The answer is that we can do something even faster by discarding all "form". Even light has a limit to its speed. By achieving total formlessness, we can travel through our thoughts from one point to another instantaneously. To do this, we must discard all notions of travel.

Southern Zen, one of a number of Chinese philosophies whose ultimate goal is the achievement of enlightenment, uses the Koan technique where a teacher or master makes a statement or asks a student a simple, but often paradoxical or seemingly meaningless question which the student may then contemplate for days, months, or years. For example, holding a club, in his hands, the master might say, "If you cannot say this is a club, and you cannot say this is not a club, what is this?" The intent of this kind of question is to break through the duality of daily life, where the normal manner of dealing with things is either by affirmation or by affirming their opposite, negation. The rational mind classifies things as A or not A and is blind to further ways of grouping its experience. For instance, the student might ask the teacher, "Have you eaten dinner yet?" and be expecting either, "Yes, I have" or, "No, I haven't".

But the teacher replies, "I just bought a new shirt for only three dollars." By analogy, the teacher is placing his hands over the student's eyes, and asking him to become more aware of his hearing, touching, and other senses.

Many Koans have accumulated throughout Chinese history which are unsurpassed for breaking asunder the mind of ignorance and opening the eye of truth. It is difficult for the Westerner to read and remember the name of the Chinese Master who told each Koan, but the lesson itself is timeless. The Koans were used by the masters to teach and enlighten the students.

The following are several famous Koans.

*   *   *   *

The master and his student sat down for breakfast but had only one cake between them.

The Master spoke. "Let us use this opportunity to see how humble we can become."

"Yes," replied the student, "and he who can declare himself most humble, shall have that one piece of cake."

"I am as lowly as a donkey," said the master.

"I am the donkey's buttocks," replied the student.

"Yes, but I am the donkey's excrement," answered the master.

"I am a maggot within that excrement," answered the student.

The master, thoughtfully, asks the student, "What are you doing in the excrement?"

"I am enjoying my vacation," answers the student.

Now the master smiled approvingly, and, while eating the cake himself, said to the student, "You have won!"

Besides its humor, this Koan carries an important lesson which careful reading and study will make clear. The comparison of donkey, to donkey's buttocks, to excrement, to maggot could go on endlessly. The master could reply that he is the maggot's buttocks, and the student could say he is the maggot's excrement, and so on.

However, to avoid this endless circular argument, the master, in his wisdom, asks the student, "What are you doing there?"

The student's reply is most clever and illustrates an important aspect of Chinese philosophy. By saying, "I am enjoying my vacation," he demonstrates that a person, depending on his attitude, can enjoy any situation. Could this insight be why the master acknowledges that the student has won? Then why did the master eat the cake?

By eating the cake, the master was breaking the student's habit of ordinary thinking, which would lead the student to expect to be given the cake. By eating the cake, the master forces the student to have a new perception of reality, and to discard all old ways of viewing life.

*   *   *   *

A student (趙州) asks, "What is Tao?"

The master (南泉) answers, "The ordinary mind is Tao." (平常心是道)

"Is there any method by which I can obtain it?" the student asks again.

"If you have the intention to obtain it, then you cannot obtain it."

"But if I give up all intention to obtain it, how can I see Tao?" the student persists.

"The Tao is beyond knowing and unknowing. To 'know' something is merely to be fooled into perceiving that you understand it. (妄覺) 'Unknowing' means that one is ignorant about the subject. To obtain Tao is to experience the void. Here are no boundaries or limitations because there are no relationships between things except for their all being part of the whole. Tao goes beyond the restrictions of knowing and unknowing and simply fills the void."

The student realized the meaning of knowing and unknowing, and so enlightened, his mind became like the void, which was instantly filled with Tao. (豁然貫通，證入如太虛的心境).

*   *   *   *

A person named Lee (李翱) had heard that there was a master (藥山禪師) whose manners and appearance were of the highest degree of elegance, and who was possessed of a great deal of knowledge. He went to visit the master and found him sitting beneath a pine tree with a classic text in his hand. The master's concentration on the classics was so great that he did not notice Lee's arrival.

Lee had a quick temper, and was also very impatient. He immediately became angry with the master, supposing him so arrogant as to find Lee completely unimportant. He said to the master angrily, "To meet someone in person is not as good as to hear of his reputation, (見面不如聞名)" and turned to leave.

The master laid down his book and looked up at Lee with a smile, "Sir, why do you place more value in what you hear than in what you see? (貴耳賤目)"

Lee was unconcerned with the master's sarcasm, and decided to test him. He asked, "Master, can you tell me what Tao is?"

The master pointed up with his index finger, then down, and then asked, "Do you understand?"

Lee responded, "I don't know."

"The cloud is in the blue sky and the water is in the bottle. (雲在青天水在瓶)"

Lee suddenly lost his disrespectful attitude and became enlightened.

(To the reader: have you become enlightened from this Koan?)

*   *   *   *

There once was a student (香岩) who traveled to visit a master (偽山), who at once acknowledged the student's reputation:

"I have heard that you are an extremely clever student, and that if you are asked one question, you will respond with ten different answers. If you are asked ten questions, you will respond with one hundred different answers. I also know of your great intelligence and talent as a debater. But I will ask you only one question; what is your true look, the one you had before you were conceived, the one you had before the one which your parents gave to you? (父母未生前的本來面目 .)"

The student was completely in the dark and at a loss for any explanation. He began to think about all the books he had read, trying to remember something that would help him answer this question. None of the lessons he had learned were suitible, he realized with great frustration. The books he had read were all like a picture of bread, which could never satisfy real hunger. (畫餅不能充飢)

From then on he asked the master time and again for an answer to the riddle. The master's answer was always the same. "You will blame me and complain to me later if I tell you now. Anyway, my answer is mine alone, and doesn't really matter to you. The only real answer for you is the one you find for yourself."

The student was severely disappointed. He burned all his books and said to himself with anger, "I will never read another book for enlightenment. I would rather be a free spirit visiting old temples and famous mountains."

He left and started on his trip. He came to Nan-Yang (南陽) where a famous master (慧忠國師) had once lived his life. The student decided to stay there a while. One day while working in the garden, he picked up a piece of tile and tossed it aside. It struck a bamboo staff and broke in two, making a clear, crisp snapping sound. This sound from nature awakened him to enlightenment. He immediately prepared a ritual bath, lit incense as an offering, and bowed to his master, who was far away.

"Master," the student said, "your kind and patient devotion has been more important to me than that of my parents. If you had simply answered my question when I had asked it of you, I would never have looked within myself and found enlightenment."

He wrote a hymn and sent it to his master:

一擊忘所知，更不假修持，動容揚古路，不惰悄然機

This hymn is written in ancient Chinese. It is difficult to translate, even only into modern Chinese. If we read this Koan repeatedly, we can gradually begin to understand its true meaning. However, it is not something that one person can simply tell to another. As a personal exercise for the student, when you begin to reach enlightenment, you can write your own thanks to your teacher as poetry or prose. One day perhaps you will be able to read Chinese, or a friend can translate for you. Then you can compare your own personal statement to this one written long ago.

*   *   *   *

A student (勝光) was digging with a small hand spade, when he came upon an earthworm. He cut the worm in two with the spade. The two pieces were still alive and moving. Just then the master (子湖神力禪師) passed by and saw the student do this. The student asked the master, "In which piece of the earthworm does the life exist?"

The master took the spade and tapped one side of the worm, then he tapped the other, then he tapped between them. After that, he tossed aside the spade and walked away without saying a word.

As you can see, one side of the worm is the future, the other side is the past. The space in between is the present. The master related the life of the worm to time, and then threw the spade away. He wanted the student to understand how important it is to discard one's notions of past, present and future with regard to one's existence.

The Koan of Zen can really prompt our mental development and realize our Yin aspect. But things have changed with time. Most of the Koans are very difficult for Westerners to understand. So here is a "present" Koan with explanation for readers.

If we wish to travel from New Brunswick to Princeton in N.J., we might be aware of only two routes. We might take either Route 27 or Route 1 south.

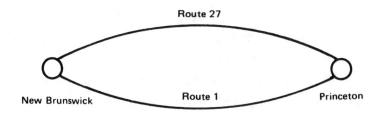

But then we find out that we can take neither Route 1 nor Route 27, because of construction, or some other obstacle. So if we still want to get to Princeton, we must find another route, by checking with maps, by asking directions of policemen or gas station attendants, etc. Maybe because of this circumstance, we will discover an even shorter way of getting there, which we never would have found if we had been able to retrace the routes that were already familiar to us. Now suppose, thought, that we are not permitted to go to Princeton by any road. Perhaps we will discover even more than just another route, something totally outside our original conception of the problem. Perhaps we will get there by going in the opposite direction, or go by helicopter or balloon or tunnel there with a garden spade. But suppose we cannot use any of these methods, or any other method we might think of. We reach a situation where we are totally helpless. We are unable to rely on any·previous knowledge or method of reasoning, beyond all knowledge, with no place to stand and nothing to hold on to. We are returning to a stage of Wu Chi. What can we do now? Our own knowledge about handling the situation is obsolete and so it is of no help to us anymore. We have become like a baby. We must start over again, without anything, completely from scratch. We must begin as a baby to learn something totally new. Before we reached this stage we were caught up in overcoming the time and space which separates New Brunswick from Princeton. Time and space were not just the obstacle that we were applying our ingenuity to, they were parts of our system of thinking about the problem. When we reach the ultimate state where our ways of thinking are useless and therefore left behind, we leave behind even the foundation of our previous thought, which was its grounding in temporal and spatial reality. This is very difficult for us to accept before we have been confronted, in some situation, with the uselessness of our present ways of knowing.

Meditation proceeds gradually and naturally to bring us into the new ways of knowing necessary to our growth in that enlightenment.

☯ 3-2 The First Stage of Enlightenment

In the previous section we discussed how meditation, unlike traditional forms of education, does not involve accumulating more knowledge, but rather involves "letting go" of knowledge previously acquired. To understand meditation as the process of letting go, we must recognize that every person is born with a kind of "mental space," an inner area of the mind for peaceful contemplation. As we age and our life becomes involved with our daily routines, we tend to fill this mental space with unnecessary or inappropriate information, such as thoughts concerning relationships, employment anxieties and our plans for the future. This type of information develops, accumulates and is stored throughout the years as a by-product of our environment which includes family, education and our imaginings.

Because our mental space becomes satiated with matters concerning daily existence, we have a tendency to place great importance on such matters and become rigid in our ways. In other words, we tend to hold onto those ideas which are stored away in our mental space and in so doing we must necessarily resist new ideas. Consider the stereotype of a senior citizen, seen as one set in his ways and conservation by nature. By analogy, the older one becomes — the more crowded becomes his mental space. Consequently, there is no room for anything new.

Meditation techniques are used to clear the mental space and to allow the mind to experience peaceful contemplation. In Taoist terms, meditation is a return to the stage known as Wu-chi or the void. Upon return to the void one develops a totally new way of thinking and in this way finds the "Yin aspects" of existence.

The process of cleaning ones mental space can be compared to the process of cleaning out a room that is cluttered with possessions acquired over the years. It is not unusual to accumulate possessions and after severval years of haphazardly purchasing such possessions, finding the room in a state of disarray. Objects so acquired often do not fit the room or each other. A room like this would soon be of no practical use because one could not relax in it, walk through it, sleep in it, or eat in it. If the room continued to be used in such a manner, it would soon function only as a space in which more things were thrown.

Perhaps you can recall a time when you found your living space too cluttered and decided one rainy afternoon to finally put it in order. Remember how difficult it was to throw some things away? Although you had worn your old coat for quite a long time, you thought, just maybe you would be able to get one more winter out of it or you might have found a box full of old photographs or a carton of your child's baby toys and said to yourself, "I couldn't possibly throw that away." This process probably continued until you were able to part with some possessions and arrange the others in an orderly fashion. Do you remember a sense of contentment after you had made some order out of the chaos?

The task of discarding unwanted thoughts from the mind is of a different and of a much more difficult nature. Obviously, it is easier to throw away the old winter coat than it is to stop mourning the death of a family member. Each of us tends to hold on to certain beliefs, behaviors and attitudes for a myriad of psychological reasons.

The following Chinese story helps to explain this point. There was a prestigious man in a community who seemingly had all material desires satisfied. He had a loving family, a large house and many servants. Not content with his good fortune, he chose to seek enlightenment.

He first refused responsibility for his estate, believing it would interfere with his spiritual pursuits. He then relinquished all material wealth and gave away even his dearest possessions. Finally, he decided that he must abandon his home. Leaving everything behind except for a small bag in which he carried a few necessities, he traveled through the country seeking teachers and wisdom.

For twenty years he carried his little bag as he walked through the countryside, studying and searching for enlightenment without success. One day he sat near a clear pond and thought how nice it would be to refresh himself in the water. He took off his clothes and laid his bag by a tree. As he laid his bag down he felt a sense of relief and immediately understood why he had searched for enlightenment for twenty years without success. He thought, "I gave up my estate, my personal wealth, my home and my family, yet, for twenty years I could not give up this bag." At that moment he attained the enlightenment for which he searched. The bag, the symbol for that which one cannot give up, was his final attachment.

The bag represents a person's final attachment, the accumulation of worldly knowledge (3rd dimension) or the ego. Only when we are able to give up everything including ourselves can we be free of the attachments which clutter the mental space and keep us from a kind of spiritual freedom. The mind is cleared and returns to the state of Wu Chi only when we can make the mental leap and let go of that certain attachment which binds us to a lower existence. Indeed, each of us carries a small bag containing individual necessities and attachments, which keeps us from experiencing this sort of inner freedom. Much like the man in the story, it is very difficult for us to lay these inner attachments down.

A story from the life of Sakyamuni, better known as Buddha

(563-483 B.C.), illustrates the difficulty involved in discarding old notions and ways of perceiving the world. The story is that Buddha had an unusual pearl which appeared to be different colors when viewed from different angles.

He held the pearl up to his disciples and asked, "What color is this pearl?" Each disciple answered a different color. He then put the pearl in his pocket and held up an empty hand. "What color is *this pearl?*" The disciples responded that there was no pearl, so they could not see any color. Buddha responded with a sigh, "I showed you a very expensive pearl, and you each saw a different color. But when I show you a *real pearl,* you tell me that you see nothing at all. People are confused and see everything backwards. Enlightenment is truly a difficult thing to attain."

The story of Buddha's lengthy and arduous path to enlightenment indicates just how difficult such a task can be. Buddha was prince of a small kingdom in Central India near the Himalayan mountains, separating India and China. When he was one year old his mother died. His mother's sister, a concubine, became his surrogate mother. Later she had children of her own, and the prince learned that his real mother had died. He became very lonely and worried. When he was three, he began to read the classic works of his religion, but the more he read, the more lost he felt. Being a prince, he was required to learn martial arts. Although he was very skilled, he did not understand why he should be learning how to fight people. At seventeen, he married and became the crown prince of his country. He had a very happy marriage, yet still felt unfulfilled. His father, the king, knew that something was wrong. He filled the palace with dancing girls, music and feasting, hoping to make Buddha more like other people. In spite of his luxurious existence, Buddha felt that something was missing from his life. He continually asked himself, "Why do I live in this world? Why did my mother die? If she had not died, would I be happy? Why do people fight with each other, and not trust each other and live peacefully?" He wondered, "If everyone comes to this world to be a person, why is it that some are fortunate and have everything, like myself, while others are so poor? All these people say there is a god. If there is a god, and he is good, why does he let all the fighting and suffering continue?"

When Buddha was twenty-nine, he had his first child. He named the child a name which means "block." The child was yet another responsibility in his life which kept him from contemplating the answers to his questions. Eventually he left, abandoning his wealth, his family, and his country.

Buddha's first teacher was an ascetic. Buddha had to sleep on a bed of nails. His skin was pierced and the blood congealed, turning the skin purple. He next slept behind a fire, which nearly roasted him and withered his body, turning him a pale yellow. His teacher had him sleep with his body buried in the ground, causing his body much discomfort from the pressure and immobility, and pain from having the blood rush to his head. He had Buddha practice staring directly into the sun in the early morning to develop endurance. The teacher told him that if he suffered through all of these things, he would attain enlightenment. Buddha asked his teacher, "Why do we want to hurt our own bodies like this?"

The teacher answered, "Because we want to enjoy the wonderful paradise of heaven."

Buddha countered, "If we do all these things, you say we will enjoy life in heaven eternal. But what will happen to us if we should fail?"

The teacher became angry, "Are you afraid to work hard and suffer and practice?"

Realizing that this teacher would not help him reach enlightenment, Buddha left. At this time, his father, the king, realized that Buddha was capable of suffering and would never return from his quest to rule the kingdom. The king sent five knights, the best martial artists in the land, to protect the prince. These guards were instructed not to allow Buddha to become aware of their presence.

Buddha found a second teacher, who told him that enlightenment could be reached through meditation. It was soon apparent, however, that this teacher did not follow his own teachings. Buddha did not desire to follow a hypocrite and so he left.

The prince wandered from teacher to teacher, always dissatisfied. He did not even uncover a single clue to the answer to his questions. Finally Buddha became convinced that no one could ever help him reach enlightenment; he would have to do it himself. The answers would have to come from within. There was no other way. This realization is the foundation of enlightenment.

Buddha eventually came to a very quiet and beautiful place in the forest. His guards lived with him, because it was easier to protect and care for him there together they practiced and meditated. Buddha practiced his meditation for hours each day in his calm and peaceful surroundings. Nonetheless, he was disturbed and ill at ease. Thoughts and feelings rushed within him like waves pounding against the shore. He felt confused, tense — as if tied up by an inner knot. Outside all was calm; inside everything was in chaos. Buddha spent six years of this practice without success. Deeply disturbed that he had not found a method to return to Wu-Chi and achieve inner peace, he asked, "Why do we always have so much pain, so many worries? When we are asleep, we feel none of this. All this pain must be related to the five senses." Buddha asked, "How can we relieve ourselves from this pain and anxiety?"

One day before dawn, Buddha arose from meditation and walked down to the riverside. A deep fog had settled over the area. As he reached the bank of the river, the sun began to rise over the horizon and the land was flooded with a wonderous display of light and color.

> Too tight, the string will surely break
> With strings too loose, there can never be made any kind of sound.
> Right tension, and a perfect chord they will make
> Which all can follow and together dance to the music they've found.

Buddha stopped and listened to this song, coming from the opposite side of the river. For the first time in his life, he appreciated its true meaning. He said to himself "It is true. You canot have the strings too tight or too loose. The tension must be right to strike the proper chord." The same relationship must exist between yin and yang to form a Tai-Chi. The song was like a light in the darkness of night for Buddha. Suddenly he could see everything very clearly. He realized that what his parents had given to him was only a body. His consciousness or awareness did not come from his parents. He likened the body to a boat, and the awareness to the captain of the boat who controls its course. When the body dies, it is merely like a boat which was been destroyed; the captain singly finds another boat and continues on its course. Buddha believed that while bodies may die, the consciousness continues on in other bodies. This is his theory of reincarnation. The consciousness controls the five senses. The five senses are the channels through which all pain, anxiety and worry enter the mind. To control and eliminate this pain, Buddha realized that we must control the consciousness or discover our own Yin-aspect.

The lesson of Buddha may be better understood in terms of everyday experiences. For example, although one might play basketball or tennis for three hours and feel happy and exhilarated, three hours of the equivalent in physical labor such as digging or moving things is joy less and exhausting. The difference is one of attitude taken by the participants. Similarly, many overweight people visit doctors and try special diet programs to lose weight. Clearly, if they would simply change their attitude, eat a little less and exercise a little more, they would steadily lose weight.

Returning now to the story of Buddha, we see that as Buddha reflected on his past, he saw that he had been like a ship floating aimlessly without a captain. When he realized that the only true teachers were the universe and himself, Buddha finally found his Yin aspect and reached the first stage of enlightenment. He also understood that he had a very heavy burden to carry a long way. He had to teach other people what he had learned: most important was the attitude of the consciousness.

All of Buddha's worries and pain were suddenly gone. He felt as if the sun was shining within him and into every corner of his being. Elated and fulfilled, all of his questions were answered; he knew why we live in this world. Like the sun rising above the city, his enlightenment had illuminated everything before him and all appeared very clear. Buddha's experience teaches us that to reach enlightenment, we must depend solely upon ourselves to gain the necessary insights.

I cannot compare myself with Buddha, who reached the first stage of enlightenment. I am only a very common man, but I can share my personal experience in reaching the door through which I have begun to learn about enlightenment. Buddha heard the song about the strings and attained enlightenment, but without his many years of disciplined and arduous searching he would have but gained nothing from the song. I too have realized that it is an extremely long and difficult task to become enlightened. Nevertheless, as with anything else, those things which are most difficult to attain are always the most valuable.

I am the youngest in my family. My mother was forty-three years old when I was born. For this reason, she had very little milk from her body to nurse. At that time in China, it was believed that if a child was fed cow's milk, the child would become covered with hair like a cow. Lower class women would often offer to nurse children of upper class parents for money, but it was foolishly believed that this would produce a child with the habits and manners of a lower class person. Fearful, my mother would not allow me to nurse with anyone else or to drink cow's milk. My only nourishment was a porridge made from rice. Consequently, I became very weak and by the age of three, I could not walk. My stomach was also very weak and continued to give me significant problems until I was forty-seven years old.

During the Communist revolution in 1949 I fled from mainland China to Taiwan with my family and lost all of my wealth and possessions. The struggle to provide for my family, combined with my prior condition, and with the smoking of cigarettes since I was nineteen, resulted in my becoming very ill in 1964. Although I was only forty-seven years old, I had an enlarged heart and a collapsed stomach. I was advised by my doctors that my condition was incurable using available medication.

The foundation for my path toward enlightenment was the realization that "I was the only one who could help myself." My choice was clear: I could try to cure myself or I could give up. I stopped smoking and began to practice Tai Chi Chuan.

Gradually, I became stronger and in five years my health returned to normal. (See the introduction in, Jou, Tsung Hwa, The Tao of Tai Chi Chuan, 1981.) My life was transformed, and I realized that I had to share my experience with others, just as Buddha was compelled to teach others about enlightenment. Accordingly, the purpose of this book and my prior work to teach rather than to profit.

Teaching Tai Chi Chuan or the steps toward enlightment is more difficult than teaching intellectual pursuits, primarily because the former is experiential and the latter is not. For example, one evening I was watching a cowboy riding a wild horse on the television. The average person watching the program would think that the horse's movements were wild and uncontrolled. Because of my fifteen years of experience with Tai Chi and slow, controlled movements, I was able to see that every movement of the horse had a specific purpose. Each and every twist or turn was calculated to throw the cowboy.

I "understood" each movement the horse made and was able to see an order in the wild and frenzied motion. Although it would be possible for me to explain the purpose of each movement to you in the minutest detail, you would only understand the movement in a limited scientific way. You cannot "understand" the meaning of each movement as I do. This is because you have not yet studied movement for yourself. One can only "understand" movement through personal experience, just as no one could teach Buddha about enlightenment except himself.

Enlightenment is not immediate, nor do we become instantly

enlightened about all things. I studied movement for fifteen years before I "understood." Interestingly, at first I became enlightened only with regard to movement. While the path to each type of enlightenment corresponds to others, each must be reached in its turn. As we become enlightened to more and more things, the path becomes easier to travel. Still, it is never instantaneous, nor is it ever a total enlightenment. A single realization will not explain all things. Enlightenment comes in pieces, each of which is the result of considerable time and effort.

The first stage of enlightenment is the sense of ease, satisfaction and peacefulness from clearing the mind of excess thought. When the mind is clear, one is capable of understanding and is able to return to a stage of Wu Chi.

As previously explained in Chapter Two, the shadow only knows limited information about the drinking glass because it only has access to a particular cross-section of the plane. Through meditation we learn to generalize the example of the shadow and apply it to every day life. For example, in connection with a family argument, a person who meditates might be able to transcend the mundane qualities of the argument and comprehend how each family member is interpreting the problem on the basis of his or her personal perspective.

Meditation can help us to realize that identical information is perceived differently by different people because each person is limited by his life experience and the manner in which he is capable of understanding that information. Accordingly, all information is analyzed on the basis of personal perspective. The meditation helps us see the whole as opposed to the parts subjectively perceived. The first stage of enlightenment, therefore, fosters an open-minded attitude, an atmosphere for acceptance, an inner peaceful mind, an appreciation for personal differences and the return to a stage of Wu Chi.

第四章

如何靜坐

Meditation

4-1 Preparation

Every human activity involves preparation of an appropriate setting that creates a mood and acts as the foundation for the success of the enterprise. Our 'inner room' of the mind is usually like the outwardly cluttered room. There are many unnecessary and inappropriate things, with the result that it is uncomfortable and distracting. To prepare, we decide which things are unnecessary and remove each, one by one. This sounds simple, but is often difficult to do. But if we examine unnecessary items and remove them, one by one, and leave only what is functional and comfortable, the room before long becomes neat, orderly and pleasant to look at. It is like a vacation from "outside" to sit in such a room in our home. The bothersome and unnecessary thoughts in our mental "room" are handled in the same way of sorting them out, and this preparation takes us to a peaceful, uncluttered mind, a state of Wu-Chi.

But these cluttered thoughts come directly from our everyday lives, and so "preparation" starts there, not only when we sit down to meditate.

The most important preparation is in the body. The body is the laboratory for experimentation and work in meditation. It must be cared for properly and in the best possible condition, and the mind that is an indissoluble part of it must be clear and well-rested to match this. This means removing deleterious activities such as smoking, drinking, eating unnutritious foods, etc. These bad habits debilitate and damage the body, and interfere with clear and peaceful thoughts. But this is like cleaning the physical room indiscriminately filled with many sentimentally attached objects. Many will object and consider only "cutting down" on what they know are their bad habits. But consider the analogy to cleaning out our closet. We come to an old coat that no longer offers its best use to us. It is time to discard it. Do we consider making a start by cutting off and throwing away a sleeve and keeping the rest? We would feel this is absurd and silly, yet it is exactly the same thing as "cutting down" on a habit we do not need and that serves us badly. If we want success at meditation, we must be willing to give up the things one after another that make it difficult to meditate well. At first this must seem quite painful; any one who has ever forced himself to clean out a neglected closet or an overstuffed room knows that feeling, so we must remind ourselves that an entirely different and more pleasant feeling followed doing a good job of it.

As we undertake this immediate and most basic task of cleaning up body and mind, we must also begin to do as thorough a job in the patterns of our daily life. As the simplest example, if we stay up all night at a party with friends, we cannot meditate successfully the next day, as we will be too tired. By extension, we must examine our life and our ordering of it, remove the unnecessary commitments that add nothing to it, and thereby make it simple to allow enough time for consistent practice of meditation. Our relations with people must be ordered and controlled so as not to infringe on this time period. Our whole life must be made as clean and orderly as body and mind if we are to succeed at meditation.

The question, "How can we possibly meditate with all the things we have to do in a day?!" is often answered by advising retreat from our daily duties to a secluded place as a strategy of value. Once upon a time such an intention was easy to carry out for any one, no matter what his or her profession. Today, easy access to a quiet and secluded place is difficult to an extreme, and the great benefits of a few moments of quiet meditation occurring naturally and impulsively throughout our day are lost. This loss is much greater than we suppose, since it is the loss of what might be called our natural inheritance and birthright. It is our natural right as human beings to have this inheritance, but due to present conditions we no longer remember this. We accept daily tension and lack of personal fulfillment and view this as our natural due. We understand that to get away from it all would make things better. We take vacations, drink, watch television, and sometimes even go on a retreat to a monastary. But we still see these activities as only transitory, activities of varying duration which must always come to an end, all too soon. And often we return from a vacation more exhausted than when we left, with a Monday morning return to the daily grind looming over our heads like a threat.

With this as our present life, we must understand that it is not only helpful, or attractive, or possibly instructive to make meditation a part of our daily life, but also a practical accomplishment of the most important and powerful sort. Yet may wonder, "How can this be?" if all the ancient wisdom we retain in our great books always points to the necessity of a highly secluded life? Meditation has often been thus associated with escapism and withdrawal from the usual daily life. Many traditional meditations were practiced apart from the everyday world, in monasteries or dwellings in the high mountains. As in other cases, this separation between meditation and the worldly life was only temporary, yet just as distinct. Withdrawal from the social community into meditation provided an opportunity for simplifying our lives so that we could concentrate better on meditation, and later we might reenter the world to help others.

But what about us, who are unable to leave work and family while learning to meditate? Our life cannot be simplified in the same way as the monk's. Concentrating, even at the times of the day we set aside for sitting in meditation, is much more difficult for us than for the monk. The situation of the traditional meditation we do is like that of a wild flower. Just as the flower is constantly exposed to the vagaries of the elements, our meditation is more vulnerable to the effects of the surrounding social environment. The less hardy strains of flowers and of humans do not persevere in this situation. But the ones that do can become even stronger than those grown in the protected environment of greenhouse.

Very important in the practice of meditation is patience. Without patience, there is little hope for success. It takes a great deal of time to make progress in meditation. If we start out trying meditation only for the fun of it, we will never make progress. Only by setting goals to train ourselves, develop ourselves, finally know ourselves and our own Yin aspect — only by setting these goals and diligently and patiently nurturing them can we make progress. Just as catching a fish takes as long as it takes for the fish to bite, so it is with meditation. There is no guarantee the fish will bite today. We must simply work and accept the results when they come.

The tool for meditation is the meditation stool. It can be made from a small wooden platform about two feet square, or two and a half feet square for a large person. It can be made with four legs, the rear legs being three inches longer than the front legs for proper elevation of the spinal column to allow for comfortable, upright, seated meditation, as shown in the figure 4-1a.

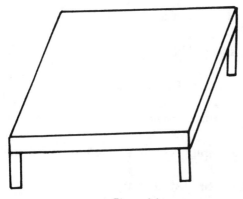

Figure 4-1a

For an easy shortcut, we can substitute books for legs and use a square board, as long as it is elevated three inches in the rear. In technologically developed countries, we may go to a lumber business that sells plywood and small beams. For a small extra charge, they will usually cut the plywood to the size desired and cut a three inch thick beam that can easily be nailed to the back of the platform to elevate it. The platform can be made in a variety of ways, such as with hinges along the center, to allow us to easily transport it for outdoor meditation or to other places. A cushion is good for sitting on the stool or we may use a folded cloth or blanket, whichever is most comfortable. Pillows are generally too soft.

Incense and incense burners are often placed nearby. For nighttime meditation, many people burn a candle. We might place nearby a pot of warm tea. The purpose is to create a pleasant and comfortable atmosphere. This way we can look forward to meditation, as if it were a vacation. Then we can take a positive attitude into meditation, and we will find it easy to pursue consistently and diligently. The secret is to make it an enjoyable experience.

Kao Pa-Lon (高攀龍), an accomplished scholar, lived in the Ming Dynasty (1386-1644). He wrote four poems describing how he enjoyed meditation during his daily life.

1. I enjoy meditating in the mountains

Time seems to roll backward

The pine tree casts a green shadow

White clouds turn slowly.

Animals have children where they'll not be disturbed

Birds make their nests in high trees;

All creatures under the sun know how to live.

Why doesn't man know this?

Sheltering within a cave, drinking spring water

Once he had very little to worry about.

我愛山中坐

恍如羲皇時

青松影寂寂

白雲出遲遲

獸窟有峻谷

鳥棲無卑枝

萬物得所止

人豈不如之

岩居飲谷水

常得心中怡

I enjoy meditating in the mountains.

2.   I enjoy meditating beside the water

Washing away the worries of the world.

It flows past and never returns.

Only a poet like me notices that.

The water is clouded with algae.

Wild flowers are now in perfection.

Fish sometimes nibble at the air.

Ducks paddle idly about

Like a stone standing in the water

I too am tranquil

我愛水邊坐

一洗塵俗情

見斯逝者意

得我幽人真

漠漠蒼苔合

寂寂野花榮

潛魚時一出

浴鷗亦不驚

我如水中石

悠然兩含情

I enjoy meditating beside the water.

3.   I enjoy meditating among the flowers

    Looking up through them to the center of sky

    The dazzling lights split into many colors

    The silver moon casts moving shadows

    Butterflies dance with joy

    Birds chirp merrily.

    A hundred ambitions are forgotten now

    Don't want to find the highest happiness.

    If you have wine, drink, and

    Feel it deep inside when holding the cup.

我愛花間坐

於玆見天心

旭日照生采

皎月移來影

栩栩有舞蝶

嚶嚶來鳴禽

百感此時息

至樂不須尋

有酒且須飲

把盞情何深

I enjoy meditating among the flowers.

4. I enjoy meditating under trees

    I feel buoyant the whole day,

    Leaning sometimes against the firmiana

    Sometimes against the pine.

    My mind is bright as a mirror

    Without worries, reflecting nothing.

    The world is green with leaves,

    As if a jade curtain were hung before gray cliffs.

    Being is blessing enough;

    This feeling, it cannot be put into words.

    我愛樹下坐

    終日自翩躚

    據梧有深意

    撫松豈徒然

    亮哉君子心

    不爲一物牽

    綠葉青天下

    翠幄蒼崖前

    撫已足自悅

    此味無言情

I enjoy meditating under trees.

Meditation twenty minutes twice a day is sufficient for the generalization of its effects into the rest of our life. However, the ordinary meditator may want more and have no other time available. The resolution of this dilemma involves the incorporation of principles from meditation into daily life. Changes in behaviour in our daily life can further the practice of sitting meditation just as much as sitting meditation benefits the rest of our life.

Su Shih (1036-1101), a very talented man, often discussed the formula of healthful living. He said, "If you're hungry, you eat; when your are near full, you stop. Then take a constitutional walk, don't let your stomach ever be too full; in fact, it's empty. Also, in your spare time, when you sit or lie down and relax, it is important that you do not move. Be like a puppet at rest. Or imagine you're sitting at the edge of Hell; if you move a little, you will fall into Hell and meet an unpleasant and fiery end. Focus your eyes on the tip of your nose, watching the breath, count each exhalation and inhalation as one; then two, three, etc., to continue endlessly. If you can count into several hundreds, with your body still, you no longer will need to imagine sitting on the edge of Hell. You will be still and have an open and peaceful mind. If you can count into several thousands, the numbers become too large. But there is another method to use at this stage, called "following". In this method, you follow the breathing with total concentration; exhale and inhale without a count. As you continue this practice, you will begin to feel the breathing through the pores of the skin. At this stage, you will become very healthy and reach enlightenment. Just as a blind man suddenly regains his sight, he can see everything by himself; you will no longer need to be guided. My words end here."

Su Shih lived about a thousand years ago, and had more leisure time and freedom than we have today. But even if we do not have enough time to practice Su Shih's method, we can still try to do something in our daily life. First, keep a peaceful mind, maintaining a meditative attitude in periods where we are not sitting in meditation.

This practice has numerous practical applications. Through practice we can learn to concentrate better on daily activities just as we learn to concentrate on a mantra, object, or point of the body in sitting meditation. That is, every time our mind wanders, we are to remember to return our attention to the task at hand. This method can enable us to clean our mental space thoughout the day. Having a peaceful mind also results from remaining centered in the midst of changing circumstances. Like the flower which bends with the wind to survive the storm, we may be flexible while at the same time sticking to what is most important. Learning not to be so influenced by other people leads to the development of a peaceful mind as well.

Another method for meditation in daily life involves the concept of control. We acknowledge the ability to control our actions in at least some situations, but emotional control presents more difficulty. If we were asked to stand up from a sitting position, anyone who was not physically handicapped could follow the instruction if they wanted to do so. However, if we were asked to change a negative emotion about a situation to a positive feeling most people would not find it so easy to comply. The control of certain gross motor movements is within the realm of our everyday experience, but emotional control is not part of our education. Sometimes we are not willing to change our emotional state, or do not know how to. In general, limitations in our thinking limit the ability to change our emotions.

The practice of meditation may eventually bring us to the first stage of enlightenment. In that stage our mind is like an empty room in which we can put whatever we want. We can control the situation no matter what happens. People may become upset briefly, but they cannot be influenced by the reactions of others.

But what does it mean to control the emotions in daily life? The first step is to become aware of our feelings and acknowledge them. Emotional control in the context of meditation does not mean surpressing or repressing the emotions. Through such methods, the emotions may appear to be under control, that is, a person seems to be calm on the outside. However, the emotions which are not properly acknowledged may build up to a point where we become exceedingly emotional; that is, severely angry or depressed. At the same time, expressing the emotions, although helpful at the beginning stage in letting off steam, is also not the aim of controlling the emotions according to meditative philosophy. Sometimes expressing the emotions in outbursts relieves the inner tension, but it only leaves us feeling more exhausted afterwards. Emotional control as the term is used here describes the process of changing Yin or negative emotions to Yang, or positive ones, not merely internalizing or externalizing our feelings. Being able to change Yin to Yang will eventually create a feeling of more, instead of less, energy. Even when we feel tired, angry or upset, we should practice controlling our emotions, and not let our emotions control us. Changing Yin to Yang is a preliminary practice to emptying our mental space.

In meditation, concentration on one or a limited number of mental devices is a way of simplifying our thinking. We can follow the same principle by making the complicated simple in everyday situations. Several examples follow. 1. Doing the best we can for others without expecting them to be grateful or to return our actions equally. 2. Throwing out the kind of thinking which we do not really need. 3. Asking ourselves if it is necessary, when we want to learn something new. Concentration in our daily life is important. If we do too many things, we won't do anything well; if we focus on one thing, we can get everything.

Many people will object to this concept, saying that it is good to try many different things. It is all right to try different things, but we should not work toward too many different goals. This merely diffuses our energy. As we become more enlightened, we realize that higher achievement in one field is really the same as higher achievement in the next.

The other method used in some forms of meditation which has applications to daily living is that of watching the source of our thinking. We are to become aware of how, when, and where various thoughts and feelings arise during the day, not only during the practice of sitting meditation. When we know the source of our emotions, it is easier to control them and not be influenced by other people or external events. One way of controlling emotions of which we have become aware is to cut them with "the mental sword," a technique similar to that of thought stopping in behaviour therapy. A more advanced method with the same purpose as finding the source involves the principle of forgetting. Instead of considering the source of a particular thought, we just forget it completely so that it has no influence.

Another unchanging principle in daily life that will change our emotions comes from the Chinese saying "Contentment brings happiness." In contrast, desire is hard to satisfy. If we are not content with things as they are, our emotion is often disturbed so that we feel upset. This emotional reaction at the same time prevents us from concentrating to change the situation, if indeed change is possible.

The goal here is not to become devoid of all feelings or human experience. It is simply to avoid extremes and maintain a balance. As we simplify our lives and focus on what is most important to us we become more content with our existences and less affected by the acts and influences of others and our emotional swings gradually subside from a gusty turbulance to the mild breeze of the wind in the trees.

Different schools of meditation teach different methods which can be classified under the following major groupings by technique. By looking at each of the different types of meditation, we can examine the parallels and better understand that which is the true essence of meditation.

1. Concentration: concentration may be either internal or external. In the external form, attention is focused on an outside object, such as a rose, a mountain top or a picture, etc. This technique is slow but safe in that there is no possibility of negative results. The

internal form is done by concentrating upon one point in the body, called Chia (竅) like Tan-Tien, a point three fingers width below the navel and two finger-widths inside of the body. This method will give much quicker results than the external method, but requires more care, since it can just as easily result in loss as in gain.

2. Contemplation: Similar to the method of concentration, this technique requires a more advanced use of the imagination. Where concentration is static, contemplation is dynamic. The meditation of the Bubble is one example which involves experiencing our thoughts as individual bubbles rising through the water of the inner self.   The bubble metaphor permits us to regulate the timing of our thoughts and to experience each thought as an individual entity. It creates a feed-back mechanism for controlling the unconscious.   Another is the Thousand Petaled Lotus method. This is a highly structured external meditation. A word or concept is chosen as the center of the lotus. Then each word or idea that flows naturally into our mind is compared and associated with the center word for four or five seconds. Then we return to contemplating the center word until the next association comes up. It can lead to insights about our inner self and the external environment, but the main purpose is to focus on the center concept. This kind of technique may result in great power, but as the possibility of gain is increased, so is the possibility of loss. To use this method of contemplation, it is advisable to practice under the guidance of an expert and accomplished teacher, since improper practice can lead to an adverse reaction.

3. Counting the Breath: This is the safest and easiest technique and may be practiced by anyone. A breath is a complete cycle of inhalation and exhalation. We either count a set of numbers such as seven, and start over, or we may count for as long as concentration permits. In either method, the important thing is that we think only of the counting and of the breath. If other thoughts disturb this, we must begin again. A similar technique is followed using the natural rhythms of the body. Find a rhythm emanating from the chest or abdomen.

Put the hands there, not to control the rate of the rhythm, but to focus meditation on it.

4. Meditation of self-inquiry: This type of meditation is a continual driving by the mind to ask itself who it really is. Each type of answer — such as a family member, a name, a sensation, a feeling, etc. — must be examined, and then rejected in search of a clearer answer as one continues to ask the question, "what is my inner self?" This is a difficult type of meditation.

5. Unstructured Meditation: This technique differs in that there is no defined structure or technique. The mind simply chooses an image, a relationship, or a concept, and actively examines and contemplates it.   The associations with any interfering thoughts are explored, then discarded. The mind must work hard to remain absorbed in the object of its focus.

6. Use of Sound or Mantra: This technique is especially helpful for those who find it difficult to concentrate, those whose minds are continually flooded with active thoughts. A common Buddhist mantra is: Namah Amitabha, (南無阿彌陀佛) which means: "I devote myself entirely to the Buddha of infinite qualities." The Taoists use a Mantra of Who, Shoe, Foo, Way, Chemmy, She, (呵 , 噓 , 呼 , 呬 , 吹 , 嘻) which not only trains the concentration, but strenghtens the body through the correspondence of each sound with an internal organ. If in a group, this is usually done by chanting the same syllable over and over, or it can be done by chanting prayers. The concentration is focused on the sound of the chanting in unison, and it is often easier to forget oneself when in a group of chanters and feel as part of the whole group.

7. Movement: Perhaps the most famous example of meditation in movement is Tai Chi Chuan. I wrote in my book, The Tao of Tai Chi Chuan (1981) that when this type of meditation is practiced. "One must give up all thoughts and become tranquil. Forget all the rules mentioned before. One must return to the primal and change the complex to the simple. Pay attention only to the Yin and Yang

changes within and without, from action to inaction, and inaction to action. Finally, find how each movement returns to its roots."

The important factor about all of these techniques is that they are all means to a common goal. Each technique is a method of eliminating or reducing thoughts which are cluttering up the mind. These are techniques for cleaning out the mental space, and just as in cleaning a room, it is not so much the way we clean it that matters, but that we gain the required result: a clean room. Each type of meditation requires the mind to focus its concentration on a single thing. This is like the process of going from Wu Chi to Tai Chi. When only a single thing occupies the mind, then the mind is prepared to forget this one thing as well and return to Wu Chi. In this way, inner peace is achieved and a new level of awareness is reached that is vivid and impressive. With meditation the primary goal is a quiet mind, and too much stress upon technique is like the man who gave up everything but could not give up his small bag. Just as he finally set down his bag, so we also must give up the technique as soon as we have mastered it. When counting the breath results in no other thoughts but those of the breath, then the method of counting the breath becomes the bag on our shoulder. We must try to set it down. When repeating a Mantra quiets our mind, then the sound becomes the burden. Set it down. Remember that although the physical process of cleaning a room is different than the internal process of eliminating a certain thought, the principle of clearing an empty space is the same. The accomplishment of such a realization is dependent upon many variables, and while natural talent may increase the probability of success, devotion to daily practice is certainly the most important element. But this devotion may itself one day become the burden we must cast off. This realization may come to our mind after five years, or twenty years, or even only after our whole life. Once we have cast this burden off, and forgotten the technique, then we have reached the edge of the first stage of enlightenment.

℗ 4-2 Chi-Kung for health

Chi-Kung or breathing meditations were developed by Taoist monks, and the term means "the use of breathing to develop the Chi for special purposes, such as fighting or healing." Chi is the energy of the universe that pervades all things, infusing each in the correct proportion. When we express an act of will, Chi is the intermediary energy that sets body and mind in motion. Although, a baby is born with a body and mind, it only comes to consciously control and understand them with experience and practice. Likewise, may an adult with serious practice, achieve perception and control of the Chi energy that is within his or her body.

Disciplined imagination is a key element in the following exercises. Children are always playing games of imagination. It expands their limited grasp of experience and "makes the invisible visible" for them. Imagination works the same way for adults.

Imagination indirectly stimulates us. For example, if we imagine that we have drunk a cup of hot coffee, the body can actually become warmer. If we imagine that we have been drinking cold spring water, it can become cooler.

Imagination can also focus conscious attention upon inner sensations and experiences that we have no words for in our common everyday language. It is through this kind of repeated and patient imagining that we eventually begin to "make contact" with the inner Chi energies. Of course, this conscious contact begins to be cultivated and built up immediately. However, meditators must practice regularly. At first nothing seems to happen and we must have the faith of a child who has planted a seed in the ground and looks each day to see if the plant has appeared!

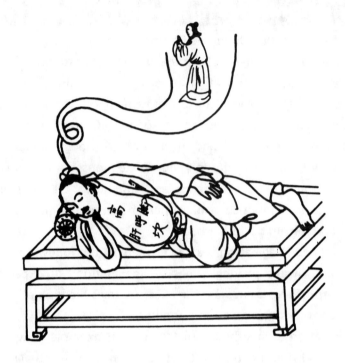

Figure 4-2a

Any comfortable and unstrained posture may be used for meditation. Through experience and practice, meditators over the millenia
have developed some postures that work better than others, or
emphasize specific effects. There are postures for standing meditation,
which include Tai Chi postures, and which are often accompanied by
very slow shifting of position (see The Tao of Tai Chi Chuan). There is
also meditation engaged in while lying down, as shown in figure 4-2a.
The meditation most widely known and which will be discussed in this
section is seated meditation.

There are three basic postures in seated meditation. The first,
San Pan (散 盤), is the relaxed, cross-legged sitting position. The
calves are crossed with the heels placed under the middle of each thigh.
The body is erect, shoulders relaxed, elbows dropped naturally
downward, and the palms placed light upon the knees, or the hands

resting comfortably on the lap. (See Figure 4-2b)

Figure 4-2b

Usually, any person can adopt this posture, although it may take a period of weeks or months before it feels habitual and completely natural. If one cannot, however, one may sit comfortably on a chair or bench. Whatever sitting position is chosen, the head and spine should be kept straight.

The next and more difficult posture is Tan-Pan (單盤) or "Half Lotus", and it requires time for the muscles of the legs to stretch sufficiently to achieve the posture. This stretching will at the same time bring the legs to a more healthy and normal degree of flexibility.

In the Tan Pan, the left leg is usually crossed over the right, with the left toes placed on top of the right knee and the right heel under the left thigh. As flexibility slowly increases with time, we can tuck the left heel into the right thigh as shown in figure 4-2c. To avoid numbness, we can alternate the position of the legs.

Figure 4-2c

There is an extremely important principle we can use in training our bodies to perform this posture comfortably, and it is a principle that applies in all physical and mental training designed to increase flexibility or energy. Go to the point where strain is felt, then back off a little bit. When this principle is violated, either there is no progress, or what progress does occur is malproportioned and incomplete.

The final and most advanced sitting posture is the Shuang-Pan (雙盤) or "Full Lotus" posture. Cross both ankles and place the heels above the knees of the opposite legs, so the soles of both feet face upward. As progress occurs, we should gradually tuck the heels further back on the thighs. We then place the right hand above the left, palms upward and thumbs connected, located on the legs near the abdomen as shown in figure 4-2d. This is the best posture in which to meditate, but again, we begin with the posture that puts the right amount of challenge to us, and then follow the progress our body makes from there.

Figure 4-2d

The following Chi-Kung postures will each send Chi to a different area of the body and make it healthier. They provide a foundation of real value for eventually developing and consciously using the internal Chi energy. Performing them will improve strength and endurance, and balance these qualities with improved suppleness and flexibility. Taken alone, they will do all these things, but they also prepare us so that one day we may advance to more difficult and more rewarding types of meditation.

Posture One.

Sitting still with a peaceful mind.

1. The optimal posture is the Shuang-Pan or Full Lotus.
2. The hands should be made into gentle, relaxed fists and placed on the thighs just above the knees with palms downward as shown in figure 4-2e.

Figure 4-2e

3.   The eyes are closed and the "mind's eye" of concentration is focused on the Tan Tien (丹田). The Tan-Tien is located three finger-widths below the navel and two finger-widths inside the body, as shown in figure 4-2f.

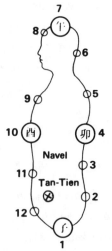

Figure 4-2f

Important Note: If the meditator is a woman and she is having her menstrual period at the time of meditation, concentration should always be focused instead on a point between the breasts and two finger widths inside the body. To focus on the Tan Tien during menstruation can result in serious harm to the body.

4. The mind is purified and emptied of all unnecessary thoughts in order to reach a state of Wu-Chi.

5. Knock the teeth. This is done by deliberately chattering the teeth together as rapidly and lightly as possible, with the mouth closed, thirty-six times or for one minute.

6. Run the tongue around the outside of the teeth, in a circle, with mouth closed, seven times. Then run the tongue along the inside of the teeth in a circle counter to the direction used on the outside, seven times.

7. There is now a mouthful of saliva. We rinse the mouth with the saliva as we would rinse it with water after brushing our teeth, but without spitting out the saliva.

8. Swallow the saliva, making a gulping sound by swallowing as noisily as possible. Follow the path of the saliva downward to the Tan-Tien with the mind's eye. Imagine and visualize the saliva turning into a steam which is the Chi, and let the Chi collect in the Tan Tien area or between the breasts if menstruating. Swallow and follow the path downward two more times.

9. Don't repeat this cycle too many times. Remember! Too much is as bad as not enough in the beginning stage. Daily practice will build up a progressive energy that no amount of excessive repetition at a single session will match.

Posture Two.

1. The optimal posture is the Shuang-Pan.

2. Very slowly and naturally lift the hands from the thighs and stretch the arms outwards to the sides, fingers uncurled and palms upward. The body remains motionless.

Figure 4-2g

3. The hands are brought together behind the head, palms facing the back of the head, with fingers interlaced and elbows pointing outward away from the body, hold back only as far as they go naturally.

4. Bring the hands to the base of the skull. The exact position is very important. The fingers are interlaced, but their tips do not reach to the base of the fingers of the opposite hand. The heel of each hand on the side of the small finger is placed against the most protuberant part of the base of the skull just behind each ear. The middle fingers cross approximately along the base of the skull. The elbows continue to be spread apart, only as far as they go naturally. The movement to this position is done slowly and gradually without any motion of the head and body.

5. Pull the abdomen inwards as we slowly inhale. This movement neutralizes the movement of the diaphragm upwards as the chest expands with air, and is an essential part of Chi-Kung breathing. As we inhale, trace the path of Chi (which we produced in Posture one, Step

8) from the Tan-Tien slowly and steadily down to point one shown in the figure 4-2f, and then up the spine along to point 4, and from there all the way to point 7 at the top of the skull. The inhalation should be completed upon reaching point 7. Hold this breath as long as is comfortable. At first we will feel this is "only imagination," but gradually we will learn to coordinate the imagination with the breathing and will be able to "feel" the areas of our body corresponding to the points.

6. Begin exhaling, simultaneously tracing the Chi back down along the chest and point 10, to the Tan Tien. As we exhale, gradually push the abdomen out so it reaches its fullest comfortable expansion as the exhalation is completed and the concentration of attention and the Chi reach the Tan-Tien.

7. The eyes are also coordinated to the exhalation and inhalation. As we begin to exhale, slowly open the closed eyes, reaching the point of their being as fully open as possible as the Tan Tien is reached. Then close the eyes, contract the abdomen slightly, and begin the breathing-contracting process, repeating the whole cycle.

8. Do this cycle 7 times.

Posture Three.

1. After Posture 2, allow the legs to stretch out, relaxing and rubbing them until they feel good.

2. Stretch the legs out forward and close together with the toes pulled backwards towards the body.

3. Slowly bend the body forward, keeping the back straight. Keep the legs locked straight, and grasp the feet with the hands, as shown in the figure 4-2h, palms inward and thumbs upward. Pull with the hands, and feel the stretching tension in the lower back. If our body has not grown supple enough to reach the feet with the hands, we may grasp the ankles or knees.

4. Inhale and contract the abdomen, following the concentration from the Tan Tien down to point 1 and up to the lower back area,

and allow the Chi to remain there.

Figure 4-2h

5. Slowly exhale and expand the abdomen as we trace the concentration and Chi back down and then up to the Tan-Tien. As we exhale, release and straighten the back simultaneously, allowing the hands to run along the legs, and reach the point of being straight upright just as exhalation is completed and concentration focuses on the Tan-Tien.

6. Reach forward and grasp the feet again, inhale, and repeat the process. Do this cycle seven times.

Posture Four.

1. Return to Shuang Pan position.

2. Contract the lower abdomen and inhale, tracing the Chi with concentration from Tan-Tien down to point 1 and then up to the back and shoulders area.

3. Simultaneously lift the hands off the thighs, separating them with fingers outstretched to trace the two sides of an imaginary circle with its bottom on the thigh and top arms-length.

4. The rising hands should reach the point of shoulder level with the palms upward and fingers outstretched just as the Chi and

concentration have reached the shoulder area in Step 2.

5.   Lift the hands overhead and interlace the fingers, then turn the palms upward as shown in the figure 4-2i.   Allow the Chi in the back and shoulders to separate and follow a path up through the arms to the fingers as the inhalation begun in Step 2 is fully completed.   Hold this position and the breath as long as is comfortable.

Figure 4-2i

6.   Slowly and naturally exhale and expand the abdomen and lower the hands in a reverse circle downward.   The Chi should be returning from each hand to the shoulders as the hands are again at shoulder level.   As we finish returning the hands to the starting position, we simultaneously complete the exhalation, complete expansion of the abdomen, and return all the Chi and concentration to the Tan-Tien.

7.   The eyes should also be coordinated to the inhalation and exhalation as in Posture Two, step 7.

8. Repeat the process, Do this cycle seven times.

Posture Five.

1. Relax and stretch the legs.

2. Return to the posture described in Posture Three: body upright and hands gently resting downard on the thighs.

3. Close the eyes. Begin the inhalation and trace the Chi and the concentration from the Tan-Tien down to point 1 and up to the shoulders. At the same time, bring the hands together behind the back, palms facing back. as shown in the figure 4-2j.

Figure 4-2j

4. Continue the inhalation, tracing the Chi down from the shoulders through the arms to the fingers. Keep the body straight. Reverse the palms away from the body and push gently outward as we complete the inhalation. Hold this position for as long as is comfortable.

5. Open the eyes. Do the entire movement in reverse while expanding the abdomen in exhalation. The palms return to touch the

back, Chi begins returning through hands and shoulders down the spine to point 1 and the Tan Tien as the palms are brought to the front and rested on the thighs.

6. Repeat seven times.

Posture Six.

1. Return to Shuang-Pan position.

2. Interlace the fingers and place them gently palms inward upon the lower abdomen, as shown in the figure 4-2k.

Figure 4-2k

3. Close the eyes, inhale, contract the abdomen and pull gently inward and upward with the hands. Hold, open the eyes, then exhale and push gently downward with the hands.

4. Upon inhalation, men should imagine that they are gently pulling their testicles upward to the Tan-Tien. On exhalation, the testicles return and the Chi travels downward and fills the scrotum. Women should concentrate on having their labia close upon inhalation and open upon exhalation.

5. Repeat seven times.

Posture Seven.

1. In Shuang-Pan, place the hands flat on the floor along side the hips, fingers forward. as shown in figure 4-21.

Figure 4-21

2. Close the eyes. Pulling in the abdomen, inhale, and trace the Chi up to the chest, simultaneously lifting the body off of the floor. (If we cannot presently achieve Shuang-Pan, there is no way of lifting our body off the floor. In this case, use our imagination to feel our body is floating in the air as we are inhaling, refraining from any movement or awkward effort.)

3. Open the eyes. Exhale and push out the abdomen as we return the Chi to the Tan Tien and lower the body to the floor. (If we are not using the Shuang-Pan, press downward with our hands and release lightly imagining the body like a balloon returning to the ground.)

4. Repeat seven times.

Note: The purpose of this exercise is to cultivate the Chi travelling between the chest and the Tan-Tien. According to traditional legends, this is the foundation of learning to feel lightness and buoyancy in the air.

Posture Eight.

Figure 4-2m

1. In Shuang-Pan, place the left palm on the bottom of the right foot, and the right palm on the bottom of the left foot, as shown in the figure 4-2m (If we do not presently do Shuang-Pan, use another position and put the palms on each knee.)

2. Close the eyes, inhale, and trace the Chi downward to number 1, and then around the abdomen in a half circle to the left that comes to the top at a point above the navel, as the inhalation is completed.

3. Open the eyes, exhale, tracing the Chi in a half-circle downward around the right side of the abdomen. The exhalation is completed at point 1. as shown in the figure 4-2n.

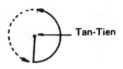

Figure 4-2n

4. Close the eyes, inhale, again tracing the Chi in a half-circle to the left up to the top point above the navel. Open the eyes. Exhale as before.

5. Make seven circles with the Chi, and on the final exhalation, return the Chi to the Tan Tien.

6. Women should trace their Chi in the opposite direction, going first from the Tan Tien to the point above the navel, then tracing downward to the left side, and upward on the right. This is due to the difference in the meridians of energy in males and females, which comes out of Yin and Yang.

Note: This exercise is especially important to the person who is learning martial arts.   It is the foundation for developing the inner energy.

Posture Nine.

Figure 4-2o

1. In Shuang-Pan, first cross the left hand and place it palm downward over the right shoulder close to the neck. Then similarly with the right hand, as shown in the figure. 4-2o.

2. Close the eyes. Simultaneously inhale and trace the Chi into the arms and shoulders. Hold the inhalation and abdominal contraction and feel the strength from the Chi filling this part of the body. Squeeze our shoulders tightly.

3. Open the eyes. Then exhale and expand the abdomen, allowing the tightened hands to relax to their original hold.

4. Repeat seven times.

Posture Ten

1. Relax and stretch.

2. Then kneel on both knees with the tops of the feet flat against the floor. Slowly sit down on the backs of the calves, with hands placed gently palms down on the thighs. This sitting position is termed Kua Ho Tso (跨 鶴坐). According to the legends, when a person became immortal, he used this position to sit on a crane's back for traveling.

Figure 4-2p

3. Place the palms of the hands on the ribcage along the bottoms of the pectoral muscles, as shown in figure 4-2p. (woman directly under the breasts).

4. Close the eyes. Inhale and contract the abdomen and allow the Chi to fill the breast area. Hold as long as is comfortable.

5. Open the eyes. Exhale and expand the abdomen.

6. Repeat seven times.

Posture Eleven.

1. Remain seated as in posture ten. Rest the hands palms downward.

Figure 4-2q

2. Close the eyes. Inhale and contract the abdomen, tilting the head, but not the body, as far back as it will go. Allow the Chi to flow upwards to fill the throat area. Hold as long as is comfortable.

3. Open your eyes. Exhale and expand the abdomen at the same time. As you are doing this, bring the head back to the normal position.

4. Repeat seven times.

Posture Twelve.

1. In Shuang-Pan position, rub the palms of the hands together until they are very, very hot. Then rub against the bare skin of the kidneys until the area feels very warm. See the figure 4-2r Keep the body straight upright. Repeat seven times.

Figure 4-2r

2. Return the fists to the thighs as in the first posture. 4-2c Close the eyes. Knock the teeth, turn the tongue, rinse with saliva, and swallow with sound as before, doing this three times.

3. If our body is weak, imagine that the saliva that has reached the Tan Tien is a fireball. Take seven inhalations and exhalations as before, tracing the burning through the circle from Tan-Tien to points 1, 4, 7, and 10, and back to the Tan Tien as before. Then feel the burning throughout the body. If you have high blood pressure, imagine instead that the saliva is an iceball and feel it cooling as it travels throughout the body to the head and back to the Tan-Tien.

(Reminder: use the point between the breasts if menstruating).

4. Sit silently with a peaceful mind as long as is comfortable.

4-3 Transfer of Ching to Chi or Lien Ching Hwa Chi (煉精化炁)

The ancient Chinese observed celestial phenomena and they found that Heaven has three treasures: the sun, the moon, and the stars. They watched the natural world and came to know that Earth has three treasures: the water, the fire, and the air. Then they asked: What are the three treasures of the body? Finally, after searching, they learned that these treasures of the body are the Ching or internal secretions; the Chi or energy; and the Shen or spirit. Ching is like the foundation of a house. It is very basic to the functioning of the body. The limited definition of Ching is sexual sperm (this corresponds also to the fluid secreted by a woman upon orgasm). The broader definition espoused by classical Chinese medical theory is that the Ching includes the essential secretions of the internal organs. This corresponds to the Western concept of the hormones that are secreted in a highly complex pattern that maintains the structure and integrity of the living body. Thus Ching is the sum total of a person's mental and physical strength, a quality that can be observed in the brightness of our eyes.

While the Ching is the body's structural integrity and cohesive strength, the Chi is the energy that animates it. If Ching were a light bulb, Chi would be the electrical energy that makes it shine; if it were a long train, Chi would be the burning fuel that powers the diesel. Ching is the organic structure and Chi is the energy that activates and maintains life. There are two major types of Chi: prebirth and post-birth Chi. There is Ching-Chi, the sperm or essential prebirth Chi, and which comes into being at the moment of conception. It is the material aspect of prebirth Chi. Then there is the prebirth Chi known as Yuan Chi, which the fetus gains from his or her mother for nourishment while in the womb. This is oxygen, nutrients, blood etc. It affects the person's development and represents the more abstract aspect of prebirth Chi. Post-birth Chi is the air which the lungs bring into the chest cavity. The broader definition includes nutritional elements. Pre-birth Chi is Yang, while post-birth Chi is Yin. These two Chis provide the basic force for maturation and life. The general term Chi combines them and thus includes food and air as well as inner energy. The Taoists discovered the secret that if we hope to live a healthy and long life, we must develop more Ching Chi from the Tan Tien again.

For the Shen (神), or spirit, there is no exact English equivalent and it is very difficult to define. The Shen is the guiding force which controls our body like the conductor of the train. Shen includes consciousness and awareness, but its influence is far more extensive than these, just as Western psychology regards that conscious acts and feelings guide and generate the organization of the subconscious. Shen is the individual's spirit, or the Yin aspect, and without it, the individual will perish.

With these three treasures of the body, plus a thousand years of practice and experience, Taoist meditation has evolved a three-stage procedure. The first stage is Lien Ching Hwa Chi (煉精化氣), or Transfer of Ching to Chi. The second stage is Lien Chi Hwa Shen (煉炁化神) or transfer the Chi to Shen. The final stage is Lien Shen Huan Shiu (煉神還虛), or to proceed from Shen to the Void, or Wu-Chi.

Lien Ching Hwa Chi is also termed "One hundred days to build a foundation" (百日築基). First of all, we must learn to intuitively regulate our sexual activities. The Chinese doctor always patiently admonishes his patients that we are not to overindulge in sex, or the loss of Ching may be detrimental.

The most important thing is not to exceed the right amount. There is no standard. Some people have more energy for sex than others. An older person has less energy for this than a younger person, and someone who is working very hard at their job cannot afford to use up as much energy as a person who is not as busy. It is not good to hold back too much either. We must seek a balance, as with everything else in life. And there is no way any one else can tell us how often is good for us. We must know this for ourselves. It is exactly the same as with food. Confucius said, "The desire for food and sex is part of human nature." We know when we are eating too much or too little at a sitting. When we are weak, we need to eat more. When we are overweight, we must eat less. It is exactly the same with sexual activity. We must find a balance for ourselves. But during the period of practicing Lien Ching Hwa Chi, it is sincerely advised that we must try to reserve as much excess sexual energy or Ching as possible, because this energy can be turned to Chi in meditation. From practicing the health-building Chi Kung, people will become stronger and healthier. Many people will experience an increased appetite for sexual activity. If this energy is all used up with increased sexual activity, they will go right back to where they began. The Chinese proverb warns, "The flying moth is forever attracted by the flame," and means the same as the English phrase "to dig one's own grave." This is why it is necessary to learn how to channel the energy of this first stage from Ching to Chi.

After long practice of the health-building Chi Kung, the student will be much better prepared for meditation. The legs will not be easily numbed, the posture will be easier to assume, the mind will be calmer, and it will be easier to concentrate. Many of these phenomena often occurring with beginning meditation, such as dizziness, discomfort, numbness, can be avoided by this diligent practice of Chi Kung. The practice of Tai Chi Chuan can also act to eliminate such difficulties.

Here, then, is the step-by-step procedure of Lien Ching Hwa Chi:

1. The student begins in the Shuang-Pan or Full-Lotus position as shown in figure 4-3a. If you cannot achieve this position, use one of the easier positions. The right hand should be placed palm upward on the open left palm, with the outstretched fingers touching, and the tips of the thumbs touching. The hands rest just in front of the abdomen. The body is erect and relaxed, with full awareness and spirit.

The eyelids are closed, but the eyes are looking as if they were open and fiercely concentrating on an object. This takes a considerable amount of practice. Make up exercises; look at an object, close the eyes and imagine oneself still looking at it, etc. Finally, close the eyes, but imagine them open and focused down inside the body on the Tan-Tien. Here again, women who are menstruating must use the point between the breasts to focus the concentration. This "looking inward" (內視) with the eyes is one of the most important ingredients for the successful practice of meditation, but very few people are aware of it, and even fewer teach it when they teach meditation.

Figure 4-3a

2. The next step is to meet the Tan Tien from below. Point one in the health-building Chi Kung exercises is the point where the giant circle of energy in the torso intersects with the path of energy that runs across the bottom of the torso. This area must be "squeezed" in a pushing upward from point one to the Tan-Tien. We must use the sexual organs and the anus to creat a gentle pressure, as if holding back when we need to urinate or defecate. We use this mild pressure

with our imagination to press upward against the Tan Tien from below, while focusing on it from above with our eyes. The Chinese use the image of a hen sitting on eggs. Our "looking inward" sight is like the hen whose body is warming the eggs, and the gentle pressure created in the point one area is like the eggs. The Tan Tien is like a nest holding everything together. So the eyes concentrate on the Tan Tien area to hatch the gentle pressure from point one. If nowadays we don't have the chance to see a hen setting on eggs, we can use the egg incubator as our example. This time the "looking inward" sight is the heat generated for the incubator to warm the eggs. This whole process is called the Yin meeting the Yang, as shown in the figure 4-3b.

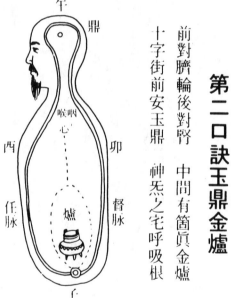

Figure 4-3b

3. We practice this at least once every day for as long as we can; maybe an hour and more, maybe only fifteen minutes. We do not force ourselves, we only give it our best.

4. Different people will take more or less time to begin to respond. It may take a couple of days, or it may take a year or more. Some people may not have any response at all. Generally, if we prepare our lives for meditation, have done the health-building Chi Kung

seriously, developed concentration carefully, and of course do not have excessive sex, then the meditation will begin to take effect more rapidly than otherwise. We will begin to feel sexually oriented sensations. Men may feel vibrations in the testicles or the prostate gland. Women may feel it as vibrations or expansions and contractions in the womb or breasts. All these phenomena are difficult to describe accurately, for language is more developed at describing exterior events. These phenomena will also vary tremendously with different people. The general term of description used by the Chinese is "Yang Chi." To excite these sensations of sex means a very crucial stage has been reached. Naturally we will be very happy if we have this sexual response, for it means we have made progress. We must treat these transient Yang Chi or sexual sensations like water and clouds passing before our eyes. Otherwise we will disrupt our concentration and cease to make any further progress. If instead we think about sexual activity, it will not only disrupt concentration but will most likely lead to increased participation in such activity. This will sap our vital energy and become a self-destructive cycle. Using such energy for increased sexual activity will make us weaker than we were before we started.

5. It is very important to control the timing in going from Ching to Chi, which is the step we will now take. If we only have a little sexual sensation or Yang Chi, we will get nothing if we try to change it to Chi. But if we wait too long for the sensations to build, it will dissipate, perhaps manifesting as a nocturnal emission the next time we sleep. The Taoist terms this Huo Hou (火候), which means the time used in cooking a certain food. One might liken it to cooking a medium steak, not too rare, not too well done. We must work out the timing for ourselves, by our feel for it.

6. When the timing is right, we inhale and contract the abdomen and imagine the breath going to point one and then both the breath and the sexual sensation travelling from there to point two, as shown in the figure 4-3c. At the same time, we follow the movement with our eyes in their "looking inward" sight. Upon reaching point two, we

relax and exhale naturally. Repeat this cycle 9 times, very gently and smoothly. Its purpose is to transmute the Yang Chi or sexual sensation to inner energy, to go from Ching to Chi.

7. If the Yang Chi or the sexual sensation remains, we follow the same cycle another 9 tiimes, only this time we go from point one to point two and finally point three. Always relaxing and exhaling naturally after each inhalation.

8. If the Yang Chi or the sexual sensation still remains, we now follow this process to point four, and then on reaching point four, keep concentrating on it for a little while, then relax and exhale. The Taoists call this procedure "Take a bath". (沐浴) as shown in figure 4-3c.

9. If we still feel the Yang Chi or the sexual sensation, this means the Ching or sexual energy has not been changed to Chi yet. If necessary, we continue the process, now as follows: a/Go from point one to four, then concentrate on point five for a while. Repeat 9 times. b/If the sexual sensation continues, go from one to four, then concentrate on point six. The total number of cycles of breath beyond the first cycle is 36. The Taoist term for this is "Inhaling to raise Yang Fire." (吸升進陽火) As shown in figure 4-3c.

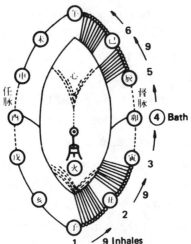

Figure 4-3c

10. If the sexual sensation or the Yang Chi still remains, we continue the process further, as follows: During the inhalation part of the cycle, trace a path from one to four, take a bath at point four, then ascend to point seven. At point seven, exhale very long and slowly, while tracing to point eight. One then inhales while focusing on point seven and again exhales to point eight. We exhale to point eight a total of six times. as shown in figure 4-3d. If further work is required, we begin tracing point one to four, take a bath at point four, trace on to point seven, then exhale to point nine, taking a bath at point ten at the end of the exhalation. Then we inhale on point seven, and complete a set of 6 exhalations. This procedure may then be repeated with 6 exhalations to point eleven, and again with six exhalations to point twelve. as shown in figure 4-3d.

The total number of exhalations in this process is 24. The Taoist term is "exhaling to descend Yin Fu." (呼降退陰符).

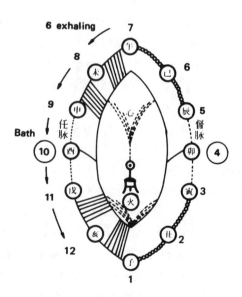

Figure 4-3d

11. We work our way through this process until the Yang Chi or the sexual sensation goes away, and to conclude it, whenever this

happens. Then we can create more Yang Chi or the sexual energy by again concentrating on the Tan Tien as we did at the start. We again follow through this process, turning the Ching into Chi. The more we do this, the more energy we will have. We will immediately feel the benefits of the energy to do something good for ourselves, or to do something good for other people. This Ching to Chi process has been developed by Taoists through thousands of years experience. It is not really a question of whether there is possible a scientific explanation of this or whether it is unscientific. The more important issue is that of self-practice. If we practice, we obtain a lot of energy from transmuting Ching to Chi. It is valuable for us to Lien Ching Hwa Chi. This method is from the Northern Taoist School (北派). Here we use our own body to transfer the Ching to Chi. In the Southern Taoist School, the method involves using a partner of the opposite sex, and very complicated sexual techniques, which will not be explored here. I will write about South Taoist meditation in another book.

Once again the crucial importance of using the Ching to transfer it to Chi and not for sexual activity must be stressed. To use it for sexual activity in this way is analogous to earning a small amount of money and immediately spending it all. This will lead to debt, or to not having the money when we need it to do something good for ourselves and others. It is most like using the money to buy drugs or alcohol, which will only destroy us. We must push all thoughts of sex out of our mind, thinking about what we are doing as a form of serious research or experiment when we change the Ching to Chi in this stage.

If it should occur that these Yang Chi or sexual sensations are not appearing, it is not a cause for despair, but understanding. It may be our body will not develop to this stage, just as some people can climb a mountain with no shortness of breath while others may never reach the top. If a person works with all of what they have and makes the most of it, their achievement and enlightenment is not of less value than that of a person who follows this method to completion. It may even be like the case of the tortoise and the hare. A person with natural endowments who follows this method easily to completion and yet practices carelessly is of lesser achievement than one who does not experience the sensations, yet cultivates and nurtures what they have to its best degree.

Also, everyone's body operates in different ways, and may not react in this way. Then we have a case of a person who "marches to a different drummer". Albert Einstein was a failure in mathematics in his primary school, yet as he aged and matured, he finally came to do things with mathematics that changed the whole modern view of the world.

Whatever our speed of progress, whether there is encouraging and pleasing experience, or whether nothing whatever seems to happen, we must continue to practice both regularly and intensively. Whether a seed is growing invisibly in the ground or whether its shoots have appeared, it needs the same nuturing. If we continue to meditate seriously, we will be gaining energy, even if we do not have the sensations. As in the proverbs, a great vessel will be long in completion and a great man or woman will take time to become sharp and mature.

The task of ignoring the sexual nature of the sensations and instead using them to transfer Ching to Chi must be pursued concertedly. This will gradually allow us to ignore and almost forget about the sensations. This is analogous to riding a bicycle. As we start to learn, we are always concentrating on our equilibrium, but after we have learned to ride, we hardly notice how smoothly we are balancing. This reflects the cycle from Wu Chi to Tai Chi and back to Wu Chi again. Creating the Yang Chi or the sexual energy and sensations is going from Wu Chi to Tai Chi. Now the trend is to forget the sensations naturally. This is a return to Wu Chi. This Wu Chi is at a different level, however. Now we have created some Chi. Gradually, we will begin to forget the sexual feelings and focus on the sensation of Chi occurring in the Tan Tien. The greater the concentration on the Tan Tien, the more we will begin to experience a new realm. It is like suddenly stepping out of the forest and into a clearing, or out of the darkness and into the light. There are no words to fully describe that kind of experience, and everyone has his or her different feeling of it. It is the same as when we see soft, bright, loveable, full moonlight; one person feels excitement, another feels quietly happy, another feels homesick and sad. It is totally an individual personal experience.

In classical Chinese medical theory, there are two important meridian lines of energy in the body. The first runs from the anus up the spine and around the top of the head to the upper lip. This meridian is called Tu (督脈) as shown in figure 4-3e. The other meridian, known as Jen (任脈), runs from the anus up to the front of the body to the lower lip. as shown in figure 4-3f. That is the reason

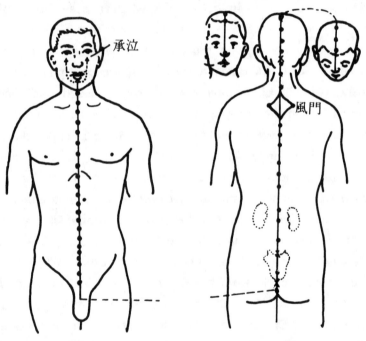

Figure 4-3f   Figure 4-3e

why when we meditate the tongue should touch the roof of the mouth to connect these two meridians. It is called Ta-Chiao (搭橋), which means to build a bridge between the Tu and Jen meridians. When we practice changing Ching to Chi daily, more Chi accumulates in the Tan Tien. Gradually we will begin to feel the energy passing through these meridians. When it can pass in a complete circle from the Tan Tien all the way around through each of the points as shown in the figure 4-3g, this is known as the Hsiao Chou Tien（小周天）or the

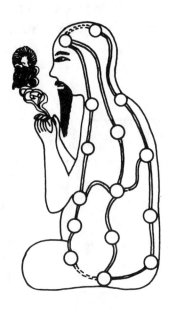

Figure 4-3g

Small Heavenly Circle. As the Chi passes through each of the points on the diagram, there is a distinct physical phenomenon which is experienced. However, each person experiences their own personal form of this. Also, when a person is not yet at this stage, it is only confusing and disturbing to discuss these phenomena. So they will not be examined in detail in this book. However, the excerpt at the end of this section from a diary describing one individual's experiences in developing inner energy may make the process more clear and easier to relate to.

If we are studying martial arts and become capable of achieving the Small Heavenly Circle or Hsiao Chou Tien, we will find ourselves suddenly far more alert, energetic, and capable of making quick progress. Those who don't study martial arts also will find that they have far more energy and become less tired, and need less sleep. The Chinese describe such a person as one who is like a live dragon or a live tiger (生龍活虎), full of vigor and vitality. The next step in the process will find the Chi traveling down the legs, to the toes, and finally out to the arms and fingers. When this is achieved, it is known as the Great Heavenly Circle or Ta Chou Tien (大周天), as shown in the figure 4-3h.

Figure 4-3h

*   *   *   *   *

In 1960 a student of meditation named Chen, a college student living in a dormitory at the time, published a diary describing his experiences with developing his Chi. Chen was unmarried and had no girl friend. The following are some excerpts from his diary:

Jan. 5

I started meditation, which I have never practiced before. I feel so much stress and tension. My legs are stiff and I cannot achieve Shuang-Pan or Full Lotus position. I used San-Pan. In ten minutes my legs were numb, and I perspired. I tried looking inward to focus concentrate on the Tan-Tien, but couldn't. I often use my hand to touch the Tan-Tien area.

Jan. 16

Recently I've felt a little better. Since the 7th, I stopped meditating after meals to avoid stomach ache. It is not a good time to meditate when I am full. My legs feel better and I've stopped sweating. My lower abdomen seems to feel like something hot is moving around, and whenever it moves, it feels very comfortable.

Jan. 24

I can feel hot Chi moving in the area of the Tan-Tien. I feel something jumping or vibrating in my abdomen, like a vibrating tuning fork.

Jan. 25

I still feel the vibrations, but it feels very strange and wonderful.

Jan. 30

Recently I have felt nothing, but today I felt the vibrating again. The skin on my legs around the hamstrings got little pimples as if from a series of tuberculosis tine tests, but they went away after a while.

Jan. 31

I felt a vibration all up and down from the Tu meridian to the Jen meridian, tracing a path of the Small Heavenly Circle of my body, as if I had gotten tuberculosis tine tests along these lines, but it wasn't painful. I also got the pimples on my legs again. It looked a little like acne and went away almost immediately.

Feb. 2

I practice meditation daily, and can feel the vibration along the Jen and Tu. I can concentrate on my Tan-Tien, but when the dormitory is too noisy. I can't concentrate, and the vibrations go away.

Feb. 3.

While meditating, I suddenly sneezed for no apparent reason. It was not cold.

Feb. 10

During dinner, I suddenly felt the vibration in my lower abdomen. I hurried back to the dormitory and sat down in a chair. I could feel the vibration in my lower abdomen.

Feb. 19

I have experienced the vibration in my lower abdomen at different times when I am not meditating. Sometimes it happens while waiting for the bus, or while reading, or something else.

Feb. 25

I had been experiencing erections at various times throughout the day. Finally, I have been able to Lien Ching Hwa Chi, to concentrate on my Tan-Tien and move the sensation up my spine during meditation. My head felt like I had a hot cap on it. It felt like there were little ants crawling around inside of my head.

March 5

There were large itchy red spots on my legs, and my penis became very hard at times.

March 7

The red spots are gone. Sometimes in class it feels like something is pulling on my heart, which is very wonderful.

March 11

My fingers vibrated during meditation. I feel a very comfortable warmth around my Tan-Tien. We played very competitive basketball for an hour, and everyone was exhausted. I felt very energetic after meditating, and was happy to be gaining benefits from meditation.

March 14

Last night my face felt like it was trembling while meditating, especially inside of my nostrils. My chest, along the Jen, was vibrating as well. I had a nocturnal emission again, but I still feel the vibration in my abdomen. It has also come to the bottom of my feet.

March 17

When I meditated in the morning, my face got very hot, and I had muscle spasms in my legs. My breathing was very deep, slow, and gentle. I held my breath for almost two minutes without discomfort. The inside of my whole body felt warm and comfortable. It felt as though there were insects crawling inside my nose and in my abdomen.

March 20

I had a nocturnal emission again on the 18th. My fingertips, face and nose were vibrating when I meditated. My penis felt itchy, and I felt like I wanted to ejaculate.

March 22.

Last night I had an erection, so I tried to draw the sexual energy up my spine and transfer the Ching to the Chi. However, I still had a nocturnal emission. My fingertips vibrated a long time. Then I could feel the Chi travel along the entire Small Heavenly Circle. At night when I meditated, I felt more saliva in my mouth. I felt something move from my ear behind my head, like an insect. I tried to brush it away, but there was nothing there.

March 23.

I still feel the vibration in my fingertips, sometimes for a long time. At night when I lay in bed, I felt the vibration in my soles, and it sometimes would move up to my toes. It made my feet itch. During meditation, it would sometimes seem as though a bright light, like a star, was passing before my eyes. In the morning, when I closed my eyes, I saw a bright yellow ring. I rubbed them and opened them, and it was gone. But when I closed them, it reappeared.

March 24

When I meditated in the morning, I felt the vibration in my abdomen, fingertips, and the soles of my feet. My scrotum had been itching during meditation recently, but that has gone away. My penis still becomes erect almost immediately. It is easier to control by concentrating on my Tan Tien now. My fingertips vibrated all day. Up until now, most of the vibrations have been in my left foot, but now it is the same in my right foot.

March 25

Between 3rd and 4th period classes this morning, I could feel the Chi move in the Small Heavenly Circle by itself very distinctly.

March 26

When I meditated in the afternoon, I felt the Chi move to my fingertips and to the soles of my feet. Suddenly, my scrotum felt itchy but in a very good way. It felt as if something came from the outside into my penis and into my testicles. It felt very good, and it was very difficult to concentrate, but I managed to focus on my Tan-Tien. I felt hot

Chi move between my testicles. My penis vacillated between hard and soft, and after about ten times, it became very soft. Then I felt a hot current of Chi run from my penis to the anus area, and then down to my legs, especially the left one. I still was concentrating on my Tan-tien. Wherever the Chi would pass, it felt very nice and comfortable.

*   *   *   *   *

Chen's progress was extremely rapid in transferring Ching to Chi within three months. He was young and very healthy, but more importantly, he was unmarried and had no girl friend. At that time in China, most college students had no sexual experience. Chen's refraining from sexuai activity allowed his rapid progress. We must temper ourselves in a similar way and not use the sexual energies we raise for increased sexual activity, or we will only drain ourselves and never make progress.

4-4 Transfer of Chi to Shen or Lien Chi Hwa Shen (煉炁化神)

When we have gotten to where we do Lien Ching Hwa Chi well and surely, it might be said "the work of 100 days is completed". For us, it may be a much different time period, since each person is different. But a time will come when we can do Lien Ching Hwa Chi well, and know it.

During this period, our whole physiology and nervous system will have become entirely different — just as the nerve impulses and muscle activity of a crippled arthritic person are measureably different from those of a healthy athlete.

Some things we may notice give an indication of the changes. Excess heat and cold no longer bother us as much as they used to. We rarely catch colds or flus or are bothered by wintertime ailments like cold feet and poor circulation. Our energy is better than before, so that the aches and pains and even the emotional miseries that come with chronic fatigue are now mostly or completely gone. If before we slept eight hours a night, now seven or even six hours leaves us better refreshed than eight used to. If we are getting older, we find that hearing and sight, instead of slowly decaying, are clear and unimpaired. Our skin will have become soft like a baby's. The way we use our eyes will be livelier and work better. People who knew us before and know us now may notice that our eyes have a sparkle they never noticed before. Our breathing patterns will be completely changed. If we can remember before how we reacted to everyday emotional crisis and how we respond now, it will seem like going from a contracted, rigid, often paralyzed style of breathing to one where the muscles of the chest are relaxed and move easily and smoothly. Often we may now notice our breathing is becoming so deep and even that we may breathe as few as three or four times a minute and feel completely invigorated with this much.

These changes that a physician or a scientist might be able to easily observe tell only part of our story. For it took us energy and great persistence to get here. Perhaps sometimes it was easy and fun, but sometimes we were so distracted and uninspired the whole thing seemed like nonsense. Yet we persisted and won. This was a matter of personal character and will, and it is a logical inference that these, too, have undergone profound changes and improvements.

As we keep doing Lien Ching Hwa Chi it increases our Yang Chi in the Tan-Tien more and more. We will tend to feel warmth in this area the whole day. When we began the exercise, focusing our awareness was all imagination. Now because of this energy in the Tan-Tien, we immediately feel the stimulation of an area when we focus our awareness in meditation.

Now there is another stage to be taken on. Without knowledge of how to maintain this energy and how to direct its use in some good way, we are incomplete. To maintain the energy we need to take up what is called pre-birth breathing, and use it to propel the circulation of energy in the Hsiao Chou Tien or Small Heavenly Circle. The Taoists liken this process to a water wheel turning endlessly through the energy of the flowing water, and call it the "secret of the three wheels" (三車 口訣) — these being the breath, the front part of the Small Heavenly Circle and the back part of it, as we can see in the figure 4-4a.

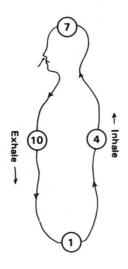

Figure 4-4a

1. While inhaling contract the stomach, and trace the awareness from point one through four and seven and down the front of the face to the mouth.

2. While exhaling, expand the stomach, and trace the awareness from the mouth down the front of the body through point ten to point one.

Keep the tongue against the front of the roof of the mouth. With practice we will feel the circulation of energy in the whole meridian like a wheel turning. We will be able to do it at any time during our everyday activities and both carry forward our training and maintain our energy.

The next circulation exercise directs the Chi up the body and out the arm, legs, and then back again; called "Chi through eight meridians."

(氣通八脉)

    1. Use the pre-birth breathing where the abdomen contracts as we inhale and expands as we exhale. Inhale and move the awareness from point one up through four to seven at the top of the head, this path is called the Tu meridian. Maintain at point seven as we hold the breath for as long as is comfortable.

    2. Exhale and expand stomach, bringing the awareness from point seven down the face and lips to point ten and finally to point one this meridian is called Jen.

    3. Inhale and imagine the awareness traveling from point one up through the inside of the body to the Tan-Tien, and from there out to the front of the abdomen where the energy divides into two paths and circles around the body, stopping at two points on either side of the spine. This circle is called the Belt Meridian (帶脉). From the two points imagine energy and awareness traveling up the back and coming to a stop at the shoulder blades as the inhalation is completed as shown in the figure 4-4b.

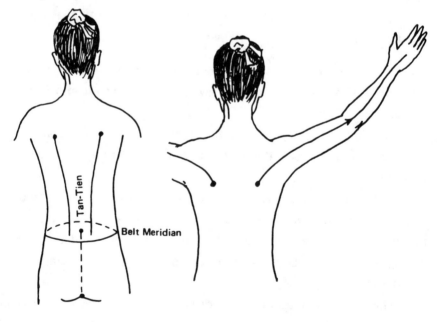

Figure 4-4b   Figure 4-4c

4. Exhale and trace the awareness from the point at the shoulder-blade over to the back of the arm and along the back of the arm, over the elbow, down over the back of the wrist and over the back of the middle finger, then down the front of the finger to the center of the palm. This path is called the Yang Yu Meridian (陽臑脉). Doing this with both paths at the same time. as shown in the figure 4-4c.

5. Inhale and trace a line of awareness along the opposite, soft side of the arm from the Yang Yu Meridian. As we reach the front of the chest move across the chest, coming to a point a little above the nipple. This is called the Yin Yu Meridian (陰臑脉) as shown in the figure 4-4d. Hold the breath at this point comfortably.

6. Exhale and trace awareness down from the two points till it reaches the belt meridian, then comes together and merges to one line at the front of the meridian, then travels inwards to the Tan-Tien and from the Tan-Tien down inside the body to point one. as shown in the figure 4-4d.

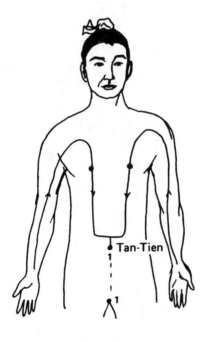

Figure 4-4d

7.   Inhale with awareness at point one, bringing it up inside the body to the Tan-Tien and then on upwards to a place just below the heart called the Chian Kung (絳宮) or Red Palace. This path is called the Tsoung Meridian (衝脉). Hold the breath here.

8.   Exhale, following the awareness down to the Tan-Tien and then to Point one, all inside the body. Continue exhaling, imagining the path dividing to follow each leg from point one to the front of the leg and then down the front over the kneecap down to the ankle and along the top of the foot, over the top of the middle toe and finally to a point on the underside of the toe corresponding to the center of the palm in the earlier exercise. This is the Yang Chou Meridian (陽蹻脉) as shown in the figure 4-4e.

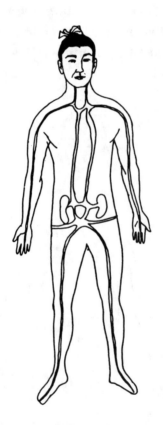

Figure 4-4e

9. Inhale and now trace awareness along the soft back part of the foot, ankle, leg, up till the two paths converge at Point one and from there to the Tan-Tien. The path along the legs is called the Yin Chou meridian (陰蹻脉). Hold the breath at the Tan Tien.

10. Exhale and trace the awareness from the Tan-Tien down to Point one. Hold the breath here.

Altogether eight meridians are used in this exercise, and they are extremely important in the circulation of energy within the body. Just as in the earlier exercises, the tracing of the awareness from point to point may at first seem pure imagination and then will come a kind of "break through" and we will be able to feel them and the flow of energy, with the perception becoming more distinct with practice.

From performing the exercise of the eight meridians over and over and circulating the Chi energy throughout the body, we will eventually come to have two experiences.

There is a point on top of a baby's head that is soft because the skull has not grown together there yet. Taoist called this point Ni Van Kung. (泥垣宮) or Pai Hui Hsuen (百會穴)

This eventually becomes a focus. As we do the eight meridians exercise, we tend to forget the body more and more and have only a sense of energy flowing where earlier we had focused awareness and imagination to attune to the experience. As this happens, our overall body comes to feel like a baby's, very soft, relaxed, comfortable.

Then, without choosing the time, we will have the experience of San Hwa Chu Ting (三花聚頂), which means three flowers coming together at the top of the head or the Ni Van Kung. We have forgotten the body almost completely, and the sense of energy that remains is now here at the top, just as earlier the Tan Tien was a lower focus.

Imagine ourselves in a dark room. Quiet. Then a skylight opens and sunshine pours in. What is our feeling? Whatever is natural for ourselves is what we will experience now. The Chinese informally term it Kai Tung (開頂) like opening the skylight.

The three flowers that come together and merge to create this experience are the Ching, the Chi, and the Shen. At first when we have this experience, we will feel our head illuminated. Gradually the illumination will fill the whole body.

We have now arrived at a stage where we may no longer focus the energy of our ego, our awareness, our will to attach ourselves to this experience and cultivate or extend its duration. To do so will fail, for we are now beyond this. Imagine a small child playing joyfully on the floor with some simple things. We see this, we want to share, we say "hello!" — what happens? The child looks at us, alarmed, startled! The joy is gone beyond recall. Any attempt to call it back by smiling, making amusing faces, only drives it further away. So we enjoy this experience without trying to do anything with it. In this way we cultivate it.

Maybe at the same time this San Hwa Chu Ting appears, maybe at a later time, comes the experience of the Wu Chi Chao Yuan (五氣朝元). Wu Chi refers to the five Chis of the body — the heart, spleen, lungs, kidneys, liver. These in turn are linked with the five primal elements — heart with fire, spleen with earth, lungs with metal, kidneys with water, liver with wood.

Suddenly, without our volition, breathing automatically ceases to occur. For a long time there is nothing. Then a very little of prebirth breathing happens.

Imagine a vast expanse of water. Imagine it directly touches all round the blue sky. There is no breeze, no waves, the sun shines. Brightness and warmth and quietness. There is nothing, nothing, nothing, yet there is a sense of everything being full of energy.

The Taoists say that the five Chis are all come to their original state of perfect harmony. That is why things are so quiet. Usually they are pulling, tugging, balancing back and forth, alternating, sometimes conflicting.

At this time we no longer understand what it is to have a body. All thoughts and knowledge have disappeared. We call life by our attachment to a body. It is gone. We call death the loss of the attachment. It is gone. What is left has everything of value it promised, and is very beautiful.

When the poet wrote his greatest lines, was it to create a beauty we would treasure and reflect back upon him, or was it to urge us to seek this place? Perhaps in our lives we recall someone saying something to us or touching us and affecting us profoundly. Now we know the gift they were urging us toward in their love, even without knowing what it was themselves. We also know more about returning the gift.

The Chinese also call this experience of meditation Ju Ting. (入定) Think of how when we read a good book, we totally forget our bodies, our physical surroundings. Imagine how when we go on vacations and climb to the high mountains we look at the clouds filling the sky, and everything is swept away. Even if someone calls to us, we do not hear. Everyone is unique and approaches this kind of experience in life in different ways. It may come even from hearing the rain fall and the wind blowing in the wet trees and feeling a sense of deep fullness and mystery.

To work in practicing these disciplines and succeed to Ju Ting is a supreme experience worth every moment and sacrifice we go to. Yet though these methods are of the greatest value, they are not unique, and this is why the person who found no progress in Lien Ching Hwa Chi should never despair, but persist in work and meditation to their fullest ability. For the Ju Ting may come to a meditator right at the very beginning of their work, or later on after failing to make progress and going on to study further. When people arrive at the mountaintop, they do not argue which path to it was most wise, but they look out over the land and the sky and are awed and quiet. And they return again and again to cultivate and evolve their sense of being.

When we arrive here, there is no longer any sense of time being intangible and ephemeral. Dreaming is a proof given to every person that our perception of time and its reality can include much more than this. In a dream, a complex emotional reality that may take months to unravel — if we are fortunate — may be resolved completely in a few seconds, and we know by our feeling it is true. Two years may pass in a flash, and a fraction of a second may expand to minutes in intricate detail.

Yet the dream is only a sample and a gift. By our work we may progress to Ju Ting where the gift is earned, and we may experience and move in the fourth dimension of time, where previously time was only a section to us that contained us as it moved. This does not mean we discard the sectional experience of time but that we bring the other awareness to it so that we experience it more fully. For example, an adult riding in an auto has a much more mature and fuller orientation to the experience than a child who merely is seeing scenes pass by rapidly. Yet both are riding in the auto and have the same raw materials to deal with.

Because of this what the Taoists call The Six Tungs (六通) becomes possible as a part of our development:

1. The Lou Chi Tung (漏盡通). This relates to sexuality, and also permits fuller understanding of why we were earlier advised to be conservative about sex and use the resulting energy somewhere else. We might• consider a small child who takes great joy with scribbles, playing with mudpies, this and that. Twenty years later he or she is doing none of these things. Why? We have nothing against these things, but have been drawn away from them by more mature experiences, because there are important things we want to do to benefit ourselves or others. Where sexuality is involved we have developed to such a degree we may do it internally without a partner using imagination. When another is involved, we find we have complete control — in the case of a man, with ejaculation; and with a female, orgasm.

2. The Tien Yen Tung (天眼通). This is called the heavenly eye. We see everything in heaven, even God, and everything on earth.

3. The Tien Erh Tung (天耳通). Here we can hear everything in heaven and on earth.

4. The Su Ming Tung (宿命通). Many people will tell you they have a sense they have lived before this lifetime and no longer remember any of it. All of this previous experience is now accessible to memory.

5. The Ta Hsin Tung (他心通). This is the complete knowledge of our future. This is not to be confused with a descendant view that human living and activity and striving are meaningless illusions not worth caring about because everything is preordained.

6. The Shen Ching Tung (神鏡通). Shen Ching means God's mirror. It means to know everything in the universe, factually. It entails the development of our knowledge about the fourth dimension.

We may think these claims are superstition and nothing else. When I started learning T'ai Chi and later meditation at the age of 47, I could never accept these, even as a person of Chinese origin. Now, years later, I cannot say I have experienced fully the six Tungs, but I have experienced a part of them. I no longer consider them as naive exaggerations or credulous self-deception. For example, I hurt my left ear while in my teens and my hearing in it was impaired. If I put a wristwatch right to the ear, I could not hear it ticking. Yet now when I meditate sometimes, at the age of 65, I will hear the faintest of sounds, such as someone speaking in a low voice two rooms away. I can verify these experiences as real and yet they represent an acuity of hearing beyond that of a normal, healthy person, and most certainly beyond that of an older person with impaired hearing.

Thus we must approach these reports from others with a mind "wide open as a valley," meditate diligently and allow experience to show us what is true. At the same time, if we wish continued progress, we must follow a Taoist warning that we not confide in others with reports of our progress and how well we are doing. If a person has something of the greatest preciousness and value, he does not brag of it to others, complacently "show off", or treat it lightly. For if he does, it is usually soon lost. The same is true here, and Taoists call the loss of further progress from this "the wrath of heaven."

Morever, these experiences of the fourth dimension are not something unique to us in advanced meditation, but are a part of the fabric of our world and are open to everyone, though without their conscious control.

Several days before he was assassinated, President Abraham Lincoln had a dream in which he was at a funeral and then heard it mentioned that he was the dead person. Many people have reported having a dream or troubled thoughts of disaster about a loved one or close friend, and later find out their premonition came just as the person was dying, or injured in an accident. While these unusual events are most often reported where the strongest emotional issues are concerned, they can often be wider in range. On our way to the mailbox we have a feeling we will get a letter from a specific friend, and sure enough, it is there. But where before this was by chance, now we develop these relations to the fourth dimension through our meditation.

The next phase in our development is the Lien Chi Hwa Shen. (練氣化神) The Taoists say that the sky has two eyes just as we do. In this stage it becomes most important to develop our eyes and sense of light. To help this, we begin by regularly practicing a set of eye exercises insure our eyes are in a state of good health. These exercises will improve weak eyesight often, and they may be added to the practicing of the Chi Kung exercises.

1. With the pad of each middle finger rub the inside corner of each eye simultaneously. Make thirty six circular motions.

Then move to the outside corners and do the same there thirty six times.

2. Curl the forefingers up so as to use the back of the second joint to rub with. Start just above the inside corners of the eye, drawing the joint softly along the muscles just above the eyeball. Continue this motion all the way out of the eye socket onto the side of the face, stopping near the ears and repeating. As with part one, the left hand does the left eye while the right hand does the right eye. Do this fourteen times.

Then start just below the inside eye corner and draw the rubbing joint softly across just below the eye, in the same way. Do this fourteen times.

3. Close the eyes. Direct them downward as far as they will go, without using excessive effort. Then downward and slightly to the right as far as they will go. Then to the side as far as they will go. And so on, tracing a complete circle, all the time trying to extend them as far as comfortably possible. Perfect doing the movement slowly and evenly as we repeat the practice. Do this circle seven times.

Then do the opposite direction seven times.

4. Close the eyes tightly, then open them as widely as possible. Do this seven times.

5. Rub hands together energetically until they become very hot. Cover the eyes with them as the eyes are kept open. This bathes the eyes in warmth and electricity from the body.

When we have done these preparatory exercises for some time and feel our eyes working adequately, we continue them, but are now prepared to begin a new kind of meditation. In the present work, we focus awareness on the Tan-Tien and the energy paths, and on the sensations of energy we perceive there. Now we begin to look instead for light. Every person's eyes have this ability to give us the vision of light that does not come from outside, and every person has had numerous experiences of this. Perhaps in bending over too long with too much strain, when we straighten up we "see stars". We look at a light bulb for a few seconds and when we close our eyes there is a glowing 'ghost' image. The inner light we will learn to see does not come from these sources, but the examples make clear to us what is meant.

From using our 'inner' eyes to focus on the Tan-Tien and energy paths, we now use them to focus on a point directly between the two eyes called the Tsu Chiao (祖竅). The Tsu Chaio is located in the valley the nose forms before it arches up to the forehead, and is just inside of the skin surface.

The secret of combining the sun and the moon (日月合併). We draw the eyes in towards the nose just as children play at "making cross-eyes," but the eyelids are closed. We do this evenly and practice doing it without excessive tension of focusing. As we do this, imagine the vision of both our eyes focused on the Tsu Chiao. This brings the complementary energies of the two eyes together, and leads eventually to our seeing the inner light.

The secret of heavenly eyes. In this different approach we imagine that we have a third eye a couple inches above the axis of our two eyes in the center of the forehead. We imagine we are looking and seeing with all three eyes, focusing on a central point called the Tien Yen (天眼) or heavenly eyes. As we practice this exercise over and over, we gradually imagine the triangle of the three eyes growing smaller and smaller. Finally it becomes such a small triangle it is a point. And that point is the Tsu Chiao.

Either exercise must be practiced as patiently and concentratedly as we did when learning to focus on the Tan-Tien and the other points. Only by working at this carefully and doing it many times did we come to sense the energy. It is the same with the light. We will come to a stage when gradually we begin to feel light coming together inside like a small full moon and can see it. As this happens we are going from Wu Chi to Tai Chi, and in our own small way repeating the cycle of the birth of the universe of something from nothing.

Now we cultivate this light carefully, we practice Hsi Chu (翕聚), which is to say we accumulate or assemble the light, so that it slowly becomes more intense and steadier. Sometimes the light will abruptly disappear. This only means we need more practice. Sometimes it may move. Here, we do not follow the movement with our eyes, but instead conclude the exercise and then begin it over again. The light that we see is named Hsuan Kuan (玄關), which means the invisible gate of the castle, and the Taoists see it as the entrance to the state of conscious immortality.

After we have learned to maintain the light strongly and

motionlessly at all times, we begin a new stage. We imagine it travelling in a small circle, and practice this over and over until we can do it well.

Then we bring the light down to the Tan-Tien and where before we felt a sensation, we now see the light. This is called Chih Tsang (蟄藏), or to 'hibernate'. Once we have become proficient at Chih Tsang and can hold the light steadily at the Tan-Tien, we then begin a rhythmical movement of the light along the Tsoung meridian upwards to Chian Kung or Red Palace, just below the heart, then from there back down to the Tan-Tien and repeat this indefinitely.

While we are doing this, we will eventually suddenly have an experience in which breathing and heartbeat almost completely stop. This is what is called Shen entering Chaio Tsung Chiao (竅中竅) and is once more an experience of Ju Ting as a different and more advanced level. We may eventually be able to remain in this state several hours, a whole day, even much longer than this.

At this stage, we speak of having created a Tai (胎), which is an embryo. The light we focus on we begin to regard as a living creature that represents the essence of our soul.

Taoists call this creation Hsin Shen Hsiang Chiao (心腎相交). They say the energies of the kidneys and the heart have merged to form a new Chien Yang (乾陽), or heavenly energy. These energy conversions can be described by the I Ching trigram method.

In the trigrams, an unbroken line represents heaven, and yang qualities; a broken line represents earthly and yin qualities. Although an orthodox Taoist scholar would decry this notion as heresy, there is also an elaborate sexual symbolism involved in which the unbroken line is taken to be the male penis, and the broken line the female vagina. This may seem unusual until we reflect that anthropologists find in every human society a complex structure of sexual symbolism in both pictorial images and in concepts about how some changes occur.

This symbolism has an important role in Hsin Shen Hsiang Chiao. Here, the image of the trigram Kan ☵ is water, and conventionally refers to the kidneys. But the trigram may also be interpreted as the female sexual organ; the unbroken line representing the clitoris, surrounded by the labia. The image of the trigram Li ☲ is fire, and refers to the heart. And the trigram Li may also be taken as the male organ — the broken line inside the trigram being seen as the passage of the penis carrying the semen. Hsin means heart and Shen means kidney in Chinese, while Hsiang Chiao means to meet together, or intercourse. Thus Hsin Shen Hsiang Chiao means the merger of the energies of the two organs in a way analogous to sexual union.

With the symbolism of the trigrams, this is thought of as the exchange of the middle line of one of the trigrams with its opposite to form the Tai or embryo, just as a couple intermingle their genetic material to conceive a child. Thus if the trigram Kan ☵ is selected and its middle line changes with the middle line of Li ☲, the Kan is transformed to Kun ☷ a feminine trigram, like a daughter, or in meditation, Yin shen. If instead Li ☲ is selected and its middle line exchange, it becomes Chien ☰, a masculine trigram, like a son, and this means in meditation, Yang shen. This change represents a profound transformation, a rebirth to a higher level of spiritual body or Fa Shen, and can be shown as in figure 4-4f.

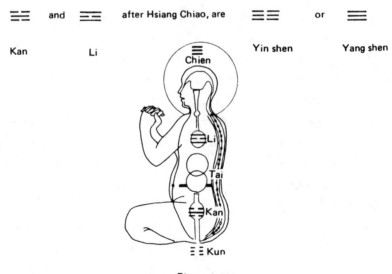

   ☵   and   ☲   after Hsiang Chiao, are   ☷   or   ☰

  Kan   Li   Yin shen   Yang shen

Figure 4-4f

4-5 Proceed from Shen to Void or Lien Shen Hwan Shiu（煉神還虛）

In Taoist theory, everyone has a physical body called the Se San
（色身）, and which is the body that doctors, pathologists, and so on
study. And everyone has a spiritual body as well called the Fa Sen
（法身）, which psychologists study some aspects of, although Taoist
studies of the Fa Sen are more advanced and go much further than
modern psychology.

We tend to experience everyday life as a whole and not divide it
up so that we are not ordinarily aware that we have actually two
separate bodies that combine to produce our everyday living. Yet this
awareness occasionally shows up. One example is the person who is
mentally ill or perhaps someone with weak nerves, neurasthenia. Such
people often experience "another body" besides their body. This
perception may also occur to a normal person at rare times in their
life when they become severely ill, perhaps feverishly delirious, or are
under severe and extreme stress. Here, too, we may encounter this
experience that we have two bodies, that our conscious attention may
be occupied in one, while we're aware the other continues to exist. The
experience of the Fa Sen we all understand is the dream where we
feel we have a body, but it is not the body laying sleeping in bed.
None of these experiences involve conscious control. Another example
is of a specially trained person, someone who has studied Tai Chi
Chuan. Such a person may be able to close their eyes and move and
control their body easily, because they can imagine or "see" themselves
with complete awareness with their inner Fa Sen body. We see this
also in the case of specially trained persons with advanced skills. For
example, a pianist may be able to control his or her playing in the same
way.

The spiritual body, or Fa Sen, has two forms; the Yin Shen（陰神）
and the Yang Shen（陽神）. The examples above relate to the Yin
Shen and involve experiences we can partly control and can experience,
but others cannot sense them. When the Yin Shen is developed to a

further degree and becomes Yang Shen, then we speak of a form of the spiritual body that others can perceive directly, just as they can see our physical body.

According to the Taoist teachings, this is one of the highest developments of meditation. The Taoists believe that our body works by the same principles as the universe. Our universe was first a void, nothing. How did it proceed from this to our moon, sun, stars, earth? We know that at some time there must have been a transition from Wu Chi to Tai Chi, or from nothing to something.

Our work in meditation has echoed this transition over and over, each time at a more advanced level. The first was our forming an intention to take up meditation and doing so. We started with the health-building Chi Kung exercises, and here we went from average or even poor health to an improved state. Then we learned Lien Ching Hwa Chi; the Chi energy of our body was improved and we learned to control it, and our health improved further.

Now we are in the stage of Lien Chi Hwa Shen (練炁化神) where we are taking the Chi energy and developing light. We began focusing on the Tsu Chaio, a very small point, just as the universe is believed to have begun as something very small. By practicing Hsi Chu, we accumulated the light into a circle like a small luminous moon.

At this stage we start to go beyond the transitory sensations of our body into something new, that these sensations carry. It is like the tale from Scheherezade and the 1,001 Nights. A fisherman nets a mysterious bottle, he breaks open its seal, and is disappointed to find only a little wisp of smoke, like incense, which emerges. But then the smoke keeps coming, and soon it is flowing out in a heavier stream. Finally it pours out copiously and as this is going on, forms a large cloud. The bottle is empty, the cloud hangs in the air, motionless, but it seems to be changing and condensing. Something is happening. The change begins to accelerate and then suddenly in an instant the form of The Genie coalesces out of this process. The Genie is a kind of folk-creature of the fourth dimensional world.

In our work, we have taken Chi energy and condensed it in a point to create the light. We used our Fa Sen to create this light from the nothing that preceded it, and the work now is the culminating stage of Taoist meditation. This is why we call it Hsuan Kuan, the invisible gateway to the castle. Once we developed this light well, we proceeded to Chih Tsang, to 'hibernate' and take this light down to the Tan-Tien and there to develop it as a Tai, an embryo.

Taoists use the image of the embryo and its development for this final level of work.

The first stage of this is called "Ten months to feed" (十月溫養), just as a mother nurtures the growing embryo in her body. We concentrate on the light at our Chian Kung or Red Palace and gradually this light grows more and more, like the Genie, and we can feel it as if it were a growing baby here as shown in the figure 4-5a.

Figure 4-5a

The second stage is called "Three years to babysit" (三年哺乳) and here the image is of a child too young and undeveloped to be out on its own and requiring constant attention.

In this stage we practice bringing the "baby" from the Chian Kung up to the Ni Van Kung on top of the head, and ultimately to a place ten inches above the head. Just as with a growing child the goal is not to get the child to do grown up things, but to supervise this naturally occurring process carefully, so it occurs in the best way. First we practice bringing the child to the Ni Van Kung from the Chian Kung. Then we begin a little bit to only imagine that it is above the head a short distance, only for a short time, and then back to the Ni Van Kung and then Chian Kung. We practice this with great care and evenness and as the weeks and months pass, we slowly increase our imagining from a very small distance above the head, to a bit more and more, till the distance of ten inches is reached as shown in figure 4-5b.

Figure 4-5b

At some time in the later stages of this work, the Fa Sen may really come out from the Ni Van Kung to the air above our head. If this happens, then we may feel the light around our Tan-Tien expand, perhaps smell something like a perfume in our nose than we can feel expand and fill the whole room, and we experience our body as being filled with a golden light.

If we reach this transition, this is a great time. And at this time we see how good our daily work has been from the start. In our daily meditations our work has been generally to have an empty body, all thoughts, all emotions calmed down like the void.

Then perhaps our Fa Sen comes out like this at a time we didn't expect, we have the capacity to feel completely unafraid, and also to feel no special happiness. If we bring things to happen this way, then it's all right.

If our daily practice has been poor and careless, then this experience could lead a person to feel so that if they look at something happy, they feel happy, and if they look at something fearful, they feel afraid. Then at this kind of time, it could also lead to the physical body being destroyed. Thus it is most important we must ask ourselves to cultivate this mood — to forget everything, forget the emotional importance of everything, forget oneself, forget other things, forget the universe — so that we see everything there, but we give nothing to it.

In this third stage of the Fa Sen being outside the body, if we really want to do well, we need nine years or more of study Lien Shen Huan Hsu (練神還虛). The Taoists say that the development may proceed in two directions —

1. When the Yang Shen leaves our body, he sees our physical body as if it were garbage and does not want to come back. A point comes when the Yang Shen is developed enough to do this, and the physical body is abandoned and dies.

2. Over a period of nine years, gradually the whole physical body becomes Fa Sen as well, and its energy is mixed together with the whole universe. It is said such a person can cause their body to dissolve like mist to nothingness, and to bring it together again like clouds forming, so that we see it as 'real'. Such a person is fully a fourth dimensional person and can moven anywhere in time and space.

Finally, let us stop and reflect. All of this may seem possible only as superstition, but what we discuss as our Yin aspect or Fa Shen that we want to develop cannot be proved as real. It is like the radio before it was invented, then it was a superstition. At that stage some person had to create the radio and build it in their mind, and then carry out the construction. For myself, I am not to this stage of development of meditation. I do not even know a person who has come to this stage. Just as we have complete control of our Yin aspect of imagination as if it were a shadow in two dimensions, it is said they have reached a further dimension of control. I cannot do this, I can only report the Taoist secrets and philosophy, and don't want to say this is 100% true or 100% superstition. I can say it is something that has been developed over a period of more than a thousand years, and there are a thousand books by different authors that report the same things.

Rather than trying to prove or disprove the experience, we try to develop methods that people can study themselves and develop themselves so they can find out directly what the truths are. This is the same as in the practice of Tai Chi, where we experience by the practice, and where the written theories are like guides or road maps to help us go in the proper direction.

In this most advanced level of Taoist meditation, we don't even think about finding a teacher. We are the teachers. From reading and hearing of the experiences of others, we can have some idea of how things might go. This approach is not so difficult as it may sound, because we have access to the Shen Ching Tung as our inner guide.

Let us review the progression of the chapter. It began with the health building Chi Kung exercises that involved strengthening of our physical body by coordinating inner energies and outer movements. At the same time we were training ourself in concentration on doing one thing. The idea is to gradually purge our mind of desires and ambitions while we are meditating, to discard all desires and worries. This is called Nien Chu (念住), and it means our thoughts and actions become more concentrated and valuable because there are fewer and fewer distractions.

Next we progress to Lien Ching Hwa Chi. Here we have no outside movement as in the Chi Kung, we have come totally to the inside. We also find the breathing coordination we begin in the Chi Kung is more important, a crucial part of the exercise. The final stage of this practice comes with our breathing getting slower and slower and finally almost stopping, Hsi Chu (息住). This is a stage of Ju Ting.

These are three distinct stages in progress, each very valuable, and we must avoid regarding stage one or even two as unimportant stepping stones to stage three. In meditation we step out of the everyday feeling we perhaps often have of needing to hurry, to get things done by a rigid deadline. We feel instead we have all the time in the world to do a thorough job, we never lose interest in making progress, yet we do not make ourselves anxious asking when the next stage will occur, or whether we are making good progress with a stage. Instead of these destructive notions, we devote our emotional concentration to performing each step thoughtfully, and we never skip steps. This is the foundation of all we do. It is most important.

Finally, we don't look for a teacher. There is more to this than just the difficulty of being 'taught' about something of an inner nature the teacher may not see. We go back to the person or persons who first discovered and wrote down the things we read of here. Who was his teacher? He had none! There is a stage in our development when we leave off having teachers, and any high achievment we come to we accomplish totally by ourselves.

Finally we undertake the Lien Chi Hwa Shen, to develop light and our Fa Sen. This eventually leads to another level of Ju Ting, where our breathing and our heart almost stops, which is called Mo Chu (脈住). The Chinese speak of this as being like a "living corpse". We no longer are attached to our body and its concerns. In this stage we are aware of everything in the universe at once, including all things past, present, and future. We have completely transcended time as a frame of reference, and one physical body has been discarded. It is analogous to living as a dream, while the physical body sleeps. Yet this dream is a reality, and we have complete control over which part of reality we will experience. ∎

THE TAO OF MEDITATION
Way to Enlightenment

Everyone can be enlightened by this inspiring and informative book. This book now makes available the basic principles of enlightenment in different forms of meditation as well as practical exercises based on traditional Chinese methods.

The book is presented in three parts:

Part One explains the philosophy of all forms of meditation. The uses of the Tai-Chi symbol and the concepts of Yin and Yang are described.

The philosophical ideas of space and time are discussed to open the reader's mind to the fourth dimension. This fourth dimensional view of our three dimensional world has never before been explained so clearly. It is truly the way to enlightenment. The need for students to create their own personal discipline is stressed.

Part Two describes in detail a series of twelve breathing exercises or Chi Kung that can be used to lead and circulate the Chi energy to every part of the body. These exercises are extremely valuable to serious martial arts students and to all who desire to reach higher levels of health and self-awareness.

Part Three deals with the Lien Ching Hwa Chi (練精化炁) or the transfer of sexual energy to psychic energy. Enlightenment through meditation is taken out of the realm of superstition and presented in a realistic, practical way. Detailed guidance to the life-long study of this traditional Chinese method, which is one of the paths leading to the fourth dimensional world, is provided.

Hardcover, 6x9. Price $15.00

THE TAO OF
I CHING
Way to Divination

For the first time in English the I Ching is presented in such a revealing light and told with such elegance through the use of pictures and vivid imagery to finally "Raise the veil of mystery" and encourage personal, practical use of this most valued work of Chinese culture.

The book describes the following:

*How the meaning of Yin and Yang evolved from the Tai-Chi diagram. The basic principles of the I Ching's structure is explained so that the student can determine the meanings of the trigrams directly from the central concept of Yin and Yang.

*Methods of divination including yarrow stalks or coins, but, most importantly, the direct interpretation of time and personal life events. You can use the I Ching to predict coming events and to adjust your behavior to attain harmony in your daily life.

*Three-part divination. The principles of the Five Elements are used for interpretation. Specific examples and exercises to illustrate each divination method are included.

*Pictures based on traditional Chinese wood block prints which are used to summarize the qualities of each hexagram visually instead of in words. This approach enhances the learning of creative, nonverbal, concepts in understanding the I Ching.

*How the traditional meanings of the hexagrams can be translated into relevant, personal terms. Included here are also many details on the lore of divination as applied to the specific hexagrams.

*As a whole, this book takes the reader away from the perception of the I Ching as a series of sayings by some wise person arrived at by a mysterious method and back to its roots as a timeless method of cultivating self-awareness and improving the quality of life.

Hardcover, 6x9. Price $20.00

Tai Chi Foundation

7199 E. Shea Blvd. Ste 109-225
Scottsdale, AZ 85254
Fax: 480 609 8663 email: Taichilj @aol.com

Name:_____

Address:_____

City:_____State_____Zip_____

____ Check or ____ Money Order Enclosed.

Yes, Please send me the book listed below:

Qty.	Code	Title	Price	Total
	To1	**The Dao of Taijiquan: Way to Rejuvenation** 7th Edition, softcover, updated information and pinyin system or romanization.	$21.95	
	To2	**The Dao of Meditation: Way to Enlightenment** Softcover. Covers theory of Daoist meditation under Northern School approach	$17.95	
	To3	**Tao of I-Ching: Way to Divination** Probably the most complete book available on the Yijing. A very intellectual work. Softcover	$24.95	
Total Order				
Shipping/Handling*				
Total Order				

* Please add $3 shipping/handling per book. Foreign orders MUST be in U. S. currency from a bank with a branch in the US to avoid service fees. Foreign order must add $12 per book airmail, or $4 per book service mail